LORDOFMESS
DEDICATED TO CATHY AND MANOU

LORDOFMESS

MY HEAD IS A VISUAL TOWNSHIP

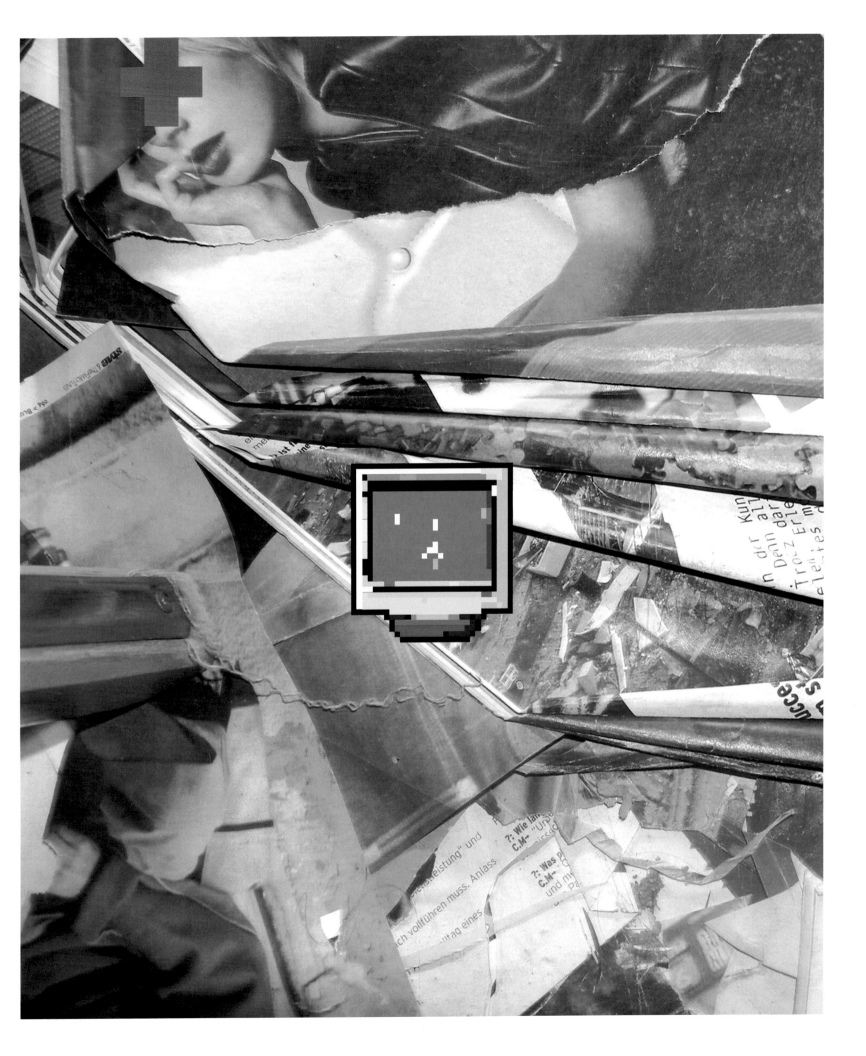

„

"My work consists of spontaneously accruing free associations. Therefore, I haven't made any attempt of cleaning my studio in the past five years. Instead I have used the layers of paper, objects, empty bottles, cigarette butts and all kinds of DIRT as my inspiration. This source of inspiration works like sediment in that souvenirs keep on surfacing and colliding with the new and the old. Whether it's computer generated or glue stick materials, digital and concrete objects fearlessly intermingle without any reserve. At the same time, every item stays raw and unprocessed. The raw bears pureness and brings balance into the chaos. For 5 years I lived immersed in my work-celluloid wildlife, video landscapes, photographic wars, Polaroid families, offset politics and fast switching – always something new on every channel and a choice of alternative visuals. These layers over layers of material play an essential role in my work, no matter what type of work it is, whether it's typography, layout or installation. My inspirations are the special qualities and emotions that I draw out of this pile of dirt. This is the idea that I want to illustrate and get across in this book." (Jaybo Monk, December 2005)

it takes a great deal of courage to embrace chaos and to work creatively while submerged in a total mess. Most people spend a considerable amount of their time on diligently managing chaos. Some even exalt the impulse to keep order as the purpose of their life. Messy situations and chaos scare us. We believe that disorder can spill over to our mental state and we would risk losing some kind of ground. Behind the chaos lurks the unpredictable, the unknown realm of infinite possibilities, yet most of us prefer to stick to the familiar. Mentally conditioned to control our environment, we limit ourselves to certain boundaries which are inevitably products of our own creation. Shedding our self-imposed boundaries and revealing the unknown fills us with fear.

At some point Jaybo Monk had decided to boldly surrender to chaos. And as a result he garnered great inspiration and wisdom in return.

Never having chosen the easy way in life, the multitalented artist has led quite a turbulent and adventurous life as an actor, musician and visual artist. Jeremie Baudouin, A.K.A. Jaybo Monk, was born in Paris in 1963. When he was 3 years old, his family moved to the quaint village of Cours de Pile in the south-western region of Aquitaine, France. There Jaybo's father, a war orphan and former military police seargent, was bequeathed a piece of land and a farm from the government. Because Jaybo's father didn't have any experience as a farmer, he recruited the family to help him with the hard work. "Already as a small child, I had to get up at 5.30 in the morning to feed the cows, milk them and bring them out to the field," Jaybo remembers, "After that I had to go to school. My school consisted of one classroom where children of all age-groups were penned up and subjected to a stern discipline. I hated school and spent most of the time staring out the window and filling my schoolbooks with sketches." Drawing has been his passion since he can remember. "It allowed me to get away from the hardships and frustration of my everyday life; it was also the only thing I found I was good at. Drawing opened up a secluded space for me where I could take refuge, where I could live out my dreams and fears by creating a world of comic characters and super heroes. Through drawing I began to perceive nature and people. It opened my mind and got me interested in understanding others as well as myself. I would draw until my hands hurt and they still hurt today." At the age of 14 Jaybo ran away from home af-

ter a dispute with his parents, and he never returned. During the following years he lived on the streets of Toulouse and later Paris. To support himself, he found work with a street theater ensemble called Royal Deluxe. While at first he assisted as a handyman, his talent for acting was soon discovered and he began performing himself. It was also in Toulouse that Jaybo first became aware of graffiti culture. He became active in the local scene known as "TALKIN'ART" initially by employing stencils and later through freehand spraying. After 3 years of street life, Jaybo hooked up with a company that specialized on returning boats to their home harbors. From the company base in Stockholm, Sweden, he sailed the seas for some 2 years until a serious boating accident detained him in a Senegalese hospital. After having recovered from his injuries, Jaybo traveled through West Africa for a while before returning back to Paris. Africa has always been a special and inspiring place for Jaybo. His close connection to African culture and people is reflected in his work. Back in Paris, he met a girl who brought him back to her hometown of Berlin. The year was 1987 and Germany was still divided. West-Berlin was a walled up stronghold in the midst of communist East Germany. After losing his passport, Jaybo decided that destiny had stranded him in Berlin. He has maintained permanent residence there ever since. "Berlin is the shit", he muses, "Berlin is the place that I love. Every time when I am away, I am missing the city. I love this village feeling about it, I love the grey. I love the cold weather and the Berlin summers. I love the inherent understatement and unpretentiousness of the city. This is the only place that gave me back the love I invested into it. Berlin has this transient vibe with a lot of people passing through, but also there are people who have never been anywhere else. It is a place where extremes clash and complement. Young and old, dirty and clean, old and new, left and right. Berlin offers opportunities that I wouldn't find anywhere else. Berlin is more than just a town; Berlin is a disguised definition of hope." In the beginning, Jaybo did street theater during the daytime and worked as a bartender at night. One day he ran into an old actor friend from France and they decided to collaborate. Together they created the celebrated cabaret show "Bürø, Bürø". Jean and Jaybo turned their lack of German speaking ability into an opportunity by producing a theater play without any spoken words, a piece that consisted entirely of onomatopoetic sounds and pantomimic gesture. There were hardly any props involved either. It was about two clerks seeking to escape their bleak office environment by dreaming about what they would rather be doing. In imagined journeys they found themselves caught up in all kinds of adventurous situations. One of the key scenes featured Jaybo mimicking a monkey. He did it with such convincing precision and authenticity that he simply flabbergasted the audience. It was around that time that Jaybo adopted the surname "Monkey" in light of the fact that the monkey was his power animal. "Bürø, Bürø" kept the audience laughing from beginning to end and it was a huge success. The 2-man ensemble went on tour and performed more than 300 times within a year. Their work was not limited to the stage as they also performed on a television show. A second play was planned but never executed. Jaybo's dread of routine and monotony prevented him from continuing with the show. Instead he ventured into gastronomy, and with a Senegalese partner he opened the Zouloubar in Berlin Schöneberg in 1991. The Zouloubar was very popular in post-wall Berlin. It attracted a hip and diverse crowd. Although Jaybo is no longer involved with Zouloubar, it continues to be a Berlin institution. After the fall of the Berlin Wall and the subsequent opening of the East, Berlin's underground club life began to thrive. Most of the clubs were illegal and were housed within many of the GDR's abandoned buildings. Jaybo was in the thick of it, actively involved in structuring club nights. He worked with the legendary clubs Globus, WMF and Boogaloo doing freestyle rap sessions, flyer design, bartending, and interior design. Different underground movements emerged in the vibrant Berlin of the early nineties, but Jaybo stayed true to hip-hop. "I tried to push hip-hop culture as much as I could to counter the techno wave that had seized Berlin in the early nineties," he recounts. In those days he also started to perform with the combo "Reality Brothers" as a rapper and percussionist. The Reality Brothers emerged from the WMF collective. Their sound was a mixture of ragga, deep soul and hip hop. Music has always been an essential ingredient in Bo's life, and besides being a skillful MC he also plays guitar, bass and percussion. Another equally successful music project he collaborated on was "Mellowbag", a freestyle hip-hop band consisting of one DJ and 3 rappers. "We had one song which was 'Illusion' that was a bigger thing. We tried to make some West Coast abstract rap, Pharcide style. In Berlin there was a lot of New York style but we tried to do a sunnier sound." Eventually, after the birth of his daughter, Manou, Jaybo quit the band to focus on things that entailed less traveling and fewer all-nighters. He continued to draw through all of this, and his hip-hop characters were very popular. One day, when he was asked to contribute one of his comic characters for a party flyer, Jaybo's friend Jahfish, a gifted DJ and graphic designer, introduced him to the computer. Jahfish got Jaybo's feet wet and he was instantly hooked on it. He immediately understood the visual design potential of the Mac. The two subsequently immersed themselves in flyer design, RAM-ing up the computer whenever they had spare money. In 1994 Jaybo co-founded the fashion-music-culture magazine "Style and the Family Tunes" with his partner Cathy Boom and their friend Christian Tjaben, A.K.A. Lunt. Because the 3 partners compliment each other so well, Style enjoys continuing success. Jaybo serves as the magazine's visual force while Cathy and Lunt comprise the fashion/business savvy and witty music expertise respectively. Since its first publication, the magazine has won several awards under Jaybo's art direction including 4 Art Directors Club awards and one Lead award. Today, Stylemag is being distributed worldwide and continues to grow without loosing any of its creative momentum and credibility. With the advent of Style's first issue, Bo began working with the now renowned fashion design collective "Irie Daily". In the beginning he provided punchy hip hop characters as print design for shirts, but later he became increasingly involved with the overall fashion design and styling. Today he is the street wear label's chief designer. When you ask Jaybo why his interests always seem to achieve a certain organic success, he humbly responds that it is not he alone but the combined efforts of people who work well and interact well together that make a project successful. "I think I am very good at motivating people. I can make them go farther, have them recognize their own creative power." The profitability of a venture is not of interest to him. He is instead constantly exploring his instinct for style in popular culture and enjoys putting the right people together to that end. "I don't think like a business man. I don't care about business. I just want to do things. And that's why it works. I'm not like 'I want to make a clothing company. I want to make a magazine. I want to make music'... I wasn't asking for it, it's just happening." Although Jaybo would never settle on only one of his multiple talents, he has increasingly focused on visual arts in recent years. During the early days of Irie Daily and Style magazine, his office was also the headquarters of a crew of graffiti artists who dubbed themselves AISM, an abbreviation for Abstractalism. "At the time when every sprayer came out to write their name on the walls as large as possible, we would do Abstractalism which meant creating new typographies that consisted of objects instead of letters. We were striving to invent our own visual vocabulary, some kind of encrypted code that nobody else could figure out, sometimes not even ourselves. It was the evolution of an iconographic typo-story." Bo's position in the AISM collective was more that of a motivator or mentor than that of an activist. He would offer the AISM crew a location to sketch out and plan for their nightly excursions and he gave them some guidance when needed. "Only occasionally I would go out with them. I was the older guy who stayed home. I didn't want to have to run when they got busted." Typography has never left Jaybo's sphere of interest. The flyer design sessions with Jahfish in his early computer days had allowed him to expand on this interest as he learned to transform, distort and slant regular types into his own customized versions. "Designing flyers for parties and concerts challenged us to match up the type with different music styles. Regardless of the genre, hip-hop, reggae or rare

groove, there had to be a link between the type and the music. I love typography because it is the most direct way to visually connect word and meaning. You can manipulate the meaning of a word by changing its typographic manifestation. Every kind of typeface tells a story. It is one of the most minimal and subliminal ways of illustration, encompassing what you can read 'between the lines'." Since around 2000, Bo has been making art under the moniker 'Monk'. The monkey has grown up. He is wiser now and his beard is turning grey. "The name 'Jaybo Monkey' was getting too well-known and my triple personality syndrome kicked in too often," he jokes," so I added a forth personality to the mix". His vast output includes oil and acrylic canvases, land-art, graphic and type design, skate board design, toy design, graffiti, installation art, computer animation and VJing. Jaybo is very reluctant about being labeled or associated with one specific technique or art form. "I never want to be a victim to the way I am doing art. It's like killing everything. Once people think they're discerning a specific technique they start with the pigeonholing, judging and comparing. I don't want to be compared. I try to direct the attention to the end result, the polished surface of my ideas and not the 'making of'. When I get tired of one way of doing things, I start doing them differently. The creative process originates in my mind and manifests itself in the art piece. Why would I restrict myself to only one way if I can imagine as many as I want?" Jaybo embraces the ephemeral nature of things in the world and is therefore not particularly attached to his work. This gives him the freedom to work outdoors, interacting with objects that are part of the common urban habitat. He feels strongly influenced by Land-art, an art form that flourished in the 1970s. The movement represented a particular version of the 'dissolving of art into life' and its objective was to evoke an imaginary world through actual transformation of nature and the real world. "I am back doing a lot of things on the street now. It's not graffiti, sometimes it goes in that direction, but otherwise it's purely installation. For instance, I carve birds out of wood and attach them to branches in trees or I throw shoes onto electro lines. I want to change the urban landscape, bring art into life to open people's eyes and minds. If someone is using the same itinerary to his job every day, I want to modify little details in this person's visual periphery and create a shift in his perception. In my territory between Neukölln and Kreuzberg, I constantly give people something new to look at. Of course most people don't see it, but when they do they will be expecting more every time. I am interacting with them, not verbally, more like I am entertaining them visually." As his main inspiration for his outside work, Jaybo references the great land-artist Andy Goldsworthy. Among the painters he admires are Robert Rauschenberg and Francis Bacon. "I like both of them for their technical skills, but generally I find every artist's work more important than the artist himself. Instead of conceptual art I prefer if an object or a situation speaks for itself. I am like a visual sponge absorbing the world that rolls out in front of my eyes. Anything has the potential to inspire me, even things that nobody wants, like discarded objects, abolished ideas or repressed emotions. In my head I am isolating small visual details to then remix them layer by layer into a new context. Essentially, the surge of images and the visual chaos in my head is where the creative process originates." Jaybo understands that what he has been searching for all over the place can only be found inside of him. At some point after all the years of experimenting and exploring the outside world, he closed the door and turned inward. This occurred at a time when he found himself in an unbearably stressful situation as the art director of Style. He was overwhelmed with projects and tight deadlines. So he decided to withdraw into his studio, declaring it as a sacred space that from now on no one, including himself, should clean up. "I sealed myself off from the exterior world in my own bubble without adding anything to what was already there. I consciously ceased expecting any new ideas or inspiration to come from the outside, only from myself. I wanted to surf my own mess. Something very important I noticed was, that when you truly want to get to know yourself, you first have to look at all your habits, all your rituals in life and everything your parents and society has imposed on you. Only when you can identify and get across all these filters and obstructions will you get to your true self." Lately Jaybo has been less and less involved in the actual graphic production of Style magazine. He has pared down his responsibilities to supervision and creative direction. Recently he founded a new graphic design company, Spread Visuals, with a few other very capable designers. Their purpose is to explore new fields of guerilla marketing and urban design. Going forward as an artist he will continue to stay true to his non-style of open ended experimentation that aims to dissolve the irrelevant divisions between art and life. Seeing urban art as a reflection of social distress and environmental problems caused by the tyranny of consumerism, he believes that it is the artist's responsibility to reveal and counteract these issues. One of Jaybo's next projects will take him on tour with a complete multimedia system. He intends to challenge other artists to a visual battle within the context of a performance. Among the disciplines will be drawing, painting and live VJing. With Irie Daily he is drafting a unique fashion signature line, and for the "European Capital of Culture" year 2009 in Linz, Austria he has been commissioned to paint the floor of an enormous swimming pool. Jaybo simply shrugs off questions regarding what he'd do if he had the means to do anything he wanted in art. "I would do the same things I am doing now. I don't need more possibilities because there are endless possibilities right in front of me. I rather have to confine myself to a minimum - less is more. I am just reacting to what is happening around me. I need the art blues to make my song, the debris to rebuild. Remember I am not important. I only exist when I am connected to life and everybody else. All I need is you all."

New York, March 3, 2006
Text: Isabel Kirsch Editor: Adam Nagata

PART 1

learning from the lines

REVERSED

AEROSOL | Electro Room / Flyer

AEROSOL | Buggydown / LP

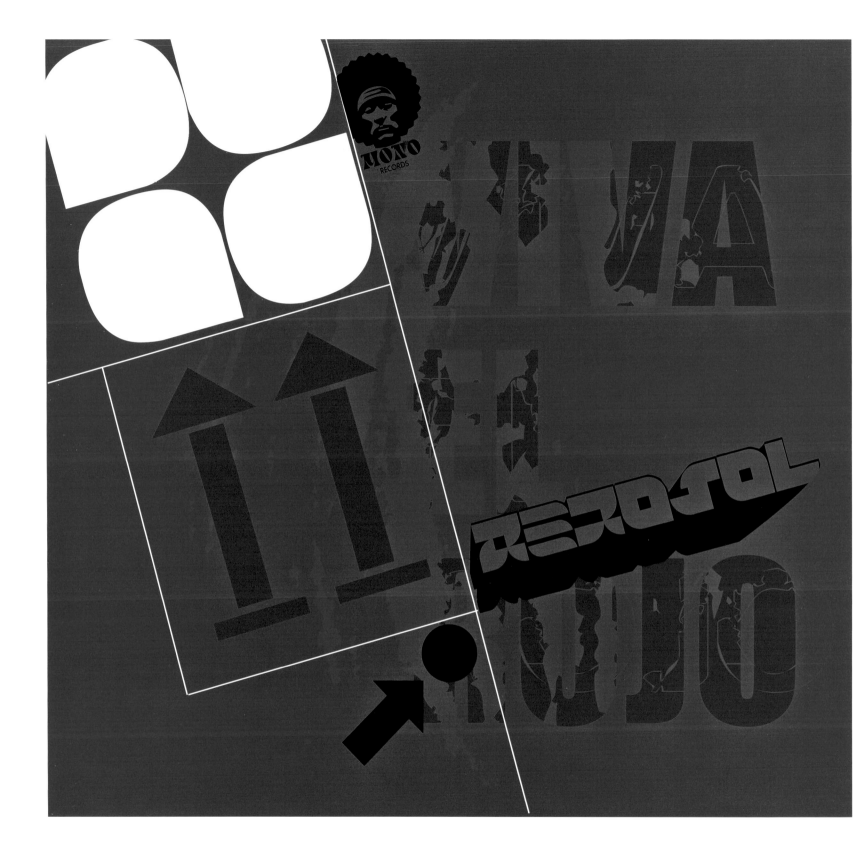

AEROSOL | Viva el Rojo / LP

Accoustic Landscape

AEROSOL

731455 97682

MONO RECORDS

AEROSOL | Accoustic Landscape / LP

SHOP SUICIDE | Sushi Plate / LP

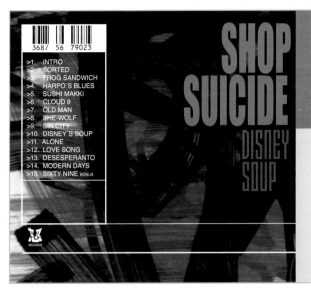

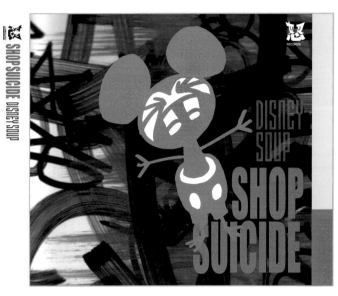

1994

SUFFRAGHETTO – SUPERSTAR

Cheryl Dunn filmt aus dem Stand die Dinge und fotografiert den Lauf einer Welt, die neben Glamour auch Gewissen haben sollte.

DIVERSATILE
MIKE MILLS

Der Mann für den Film zur Band zum Video zum Plattencover zum T-Shirt zum Bild.

"Mir gefällt die Vorstellung, dass meine Cover bei den verschiedensten Leuten zu Hause stehen. Jeder hat Platten oder CDs, und deshalb ist Cover Gestaltung eine Art Alltagskunst."

DropS by laybo

"ES HEIßT, DASS EIN FILIPINO KIND PRO STUNDE AN ARMUT STIRBT, IN EINEM LAND, DESSEN HALBER LANDESHAU... DAZU DIENEN MUSS, DIE ZINSEN AUF KREDITE DER WELTBANK UND DES IWF ZU DECKEN." John Pilger, Hidden Agendas

Drop The Debt

> Was haben U2´s Bono, Muhammad Ali, Radiohead´s Thom Yorke und der Dalai Lama gemeinsam? Sie alle benutzen ihre Popularität, um gegen die Verschuldung der Dritten Welt zu protestieren. Sie unterstützen damit den Aktion Tausender Menschen aus der ganzen Welt, die sich ebenfalls in der "Jubilee 2000" engagieren. Um auf das Verschuldungs-Thema aufmerksam zu machen und den Erlass der Schulden einzufordern, hat das Dazed&Confused Magazin Texte und Bilder zusammengestellt, von denen wir hier eine Auswahl veröffentlichen.

> Am 26.09. findet in Prag das jährliche Meeting von Weltbank und IWF statt. Umgeben von ca. 11.000 Polizisten und einer eigens eingerichteten Außenstelle des FBI werden die größten Protestaktionen seit Seattle erwartet. Der Kern der Forderungen ist der Ruf nach der Entschuldung der Dritten Welt. Die Teilnahme an der Email Aktion zum Erlassjahr, das Verschicken der umseitig abgedruckten Petition oder die Beteiligung an den Protesten auf den Strassen Prags sind Möglichkeiten, sich an der Kampagne zu beteiligen, um der Dritte Welt Verschuldung ein Ende zu machen.

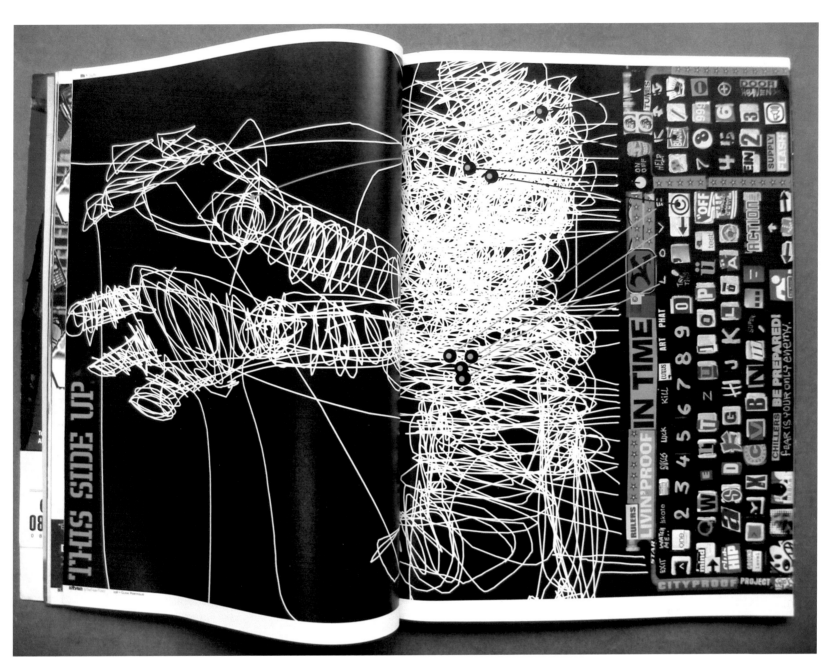

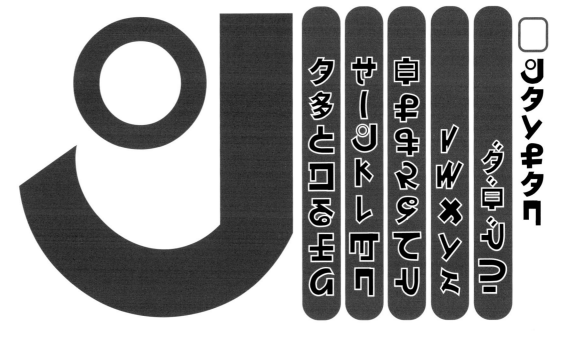

THIS IS THE TIGHT ISSUE THIS IS THE TIGHT ISSUE THIS IS THE TIGHT ISSUE THIS IS THE TIGHT ISSUE THIS IS THE TIGHT ISSUE
THIS IS THE TIGHT ISSUE THIS IS THE TIGHT ISSUE THIS IS THE TIGHT ISSUE THIS IS THE TIGHT ISSUE THIS IS THE TIGHT ISSUE
THIS IS THE TIGHT ISSUE THIS IS THE TIGHT ISSUE THIS IS THE TIGHT ISSUE THIS IS THE TIGHT ISSUE THIS IS THE TIGHT ISSUE
THIS IS THE TIGHT ISSUE THIS IS THE TIGHT ISSUE THIS IS THE TIGHT ISSUE THIS IS THE TIGHT ISSUE THIS IS THE TIGHT ISSUE
THIS IS THE TIGHT ISSUE THIS IS THE TIGHT ISSUE THIS IS THE TIGHT ISSUE THIS IS THE TIGHT ISSUE THIS IS THE TIGHT ISSUE
THIS IS THE TIGHT ISSUE THIS IS THE TIGHT ISSUE THIS IS THE TIGHT ISSUE THIS IS THE TIGHT ISSUE THIS IS THE TIGHT ISSUE
THIS IS THE TIGHT ISSUE THIS IS THE TIGHT ISSUE THIS IS THE TIGHT ISSUE THIS IS THE TIGHT ISSUE THIS IS THE TIGHT ISSUE
THIS IS THE TIGHT ISSUE THIS IS THE TIGHT ISSUE THIS IS THE TIGHT ISSUE THIS IS THE TIGHT ISSUE THIS IS THE TIGHT ISSUE
THIS IS THE TIGHT ISSUE THIS IS THE TIGHT ISSUE THIS IS THE TIGHT ISSUE THIS IS THE TIGHT ISSUE

THIS ISSUE IS DEDICATED TO STANLEY KUBRICK -

INTRO

SHINE ON YOU CRAZY DIAMOND

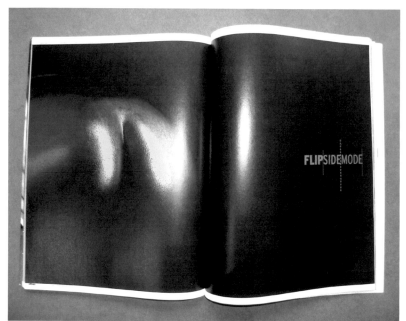

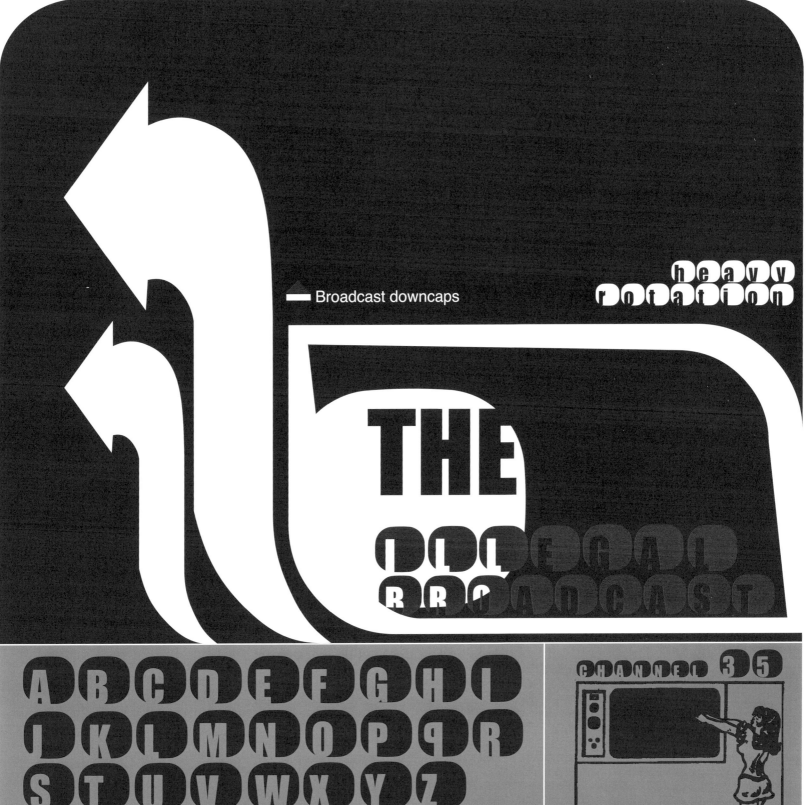

Broadcast downcaps

heavy rotation

THE ILLEGAL BROADCAST

A B C D E F G H I
J K L M N O P Q R
S T U V W X Y Z
1 2 3 4 5 6 7 8 9
AND THE ! ¡ ? ß / +

CHANNEL 35

THE Q
456

004 PULLOVER + BLUSE / BALENCIAGA
SHORTS / PRADA SPORT
BOOTS / MIU MIU

005 KISS T-SHIRT / 2ND HAND
LEDERHOSE / HELMUT LANG
SNEAKERS / GEOX

006 CUSTOMIZED SHIRT / CARHARTT
HOSE / CATERPILLAR
SCHUHE / MIU MIU

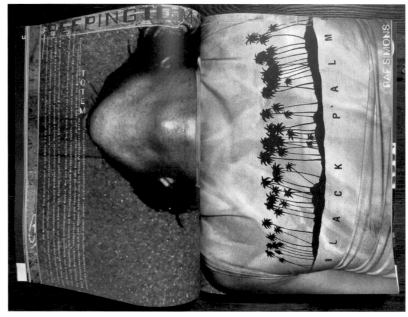
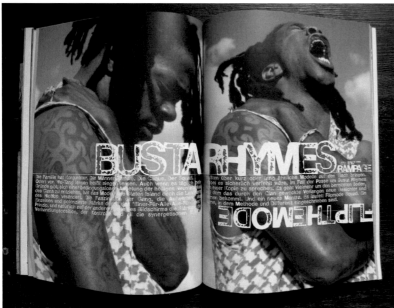

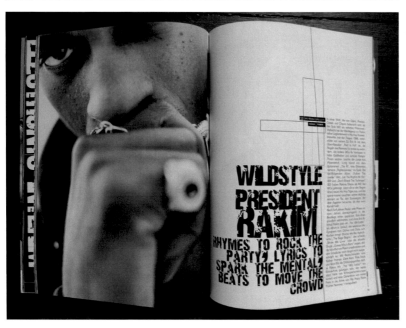
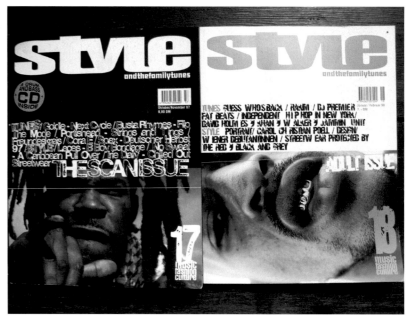

SQUARESTYLE
ABCDEFGHIJKLM
NOPQRSTUVWXYZ
ÄÖÜ1234567890

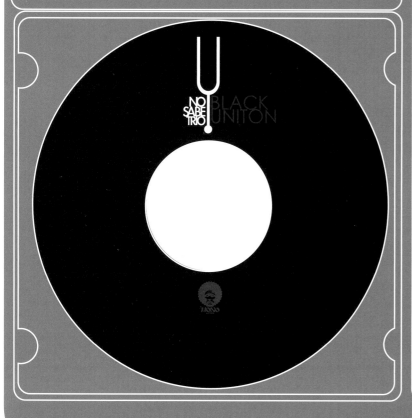

NO SABE TRIO | *Cover Tries / Black Uniton / Honey Drop*

IfeelGuilty

COUSCOUS GUITAR
AEROSOL
NO SABE TRIO

10.05.04 @AZUCAR BOX 2300pm 114 rua del liberation

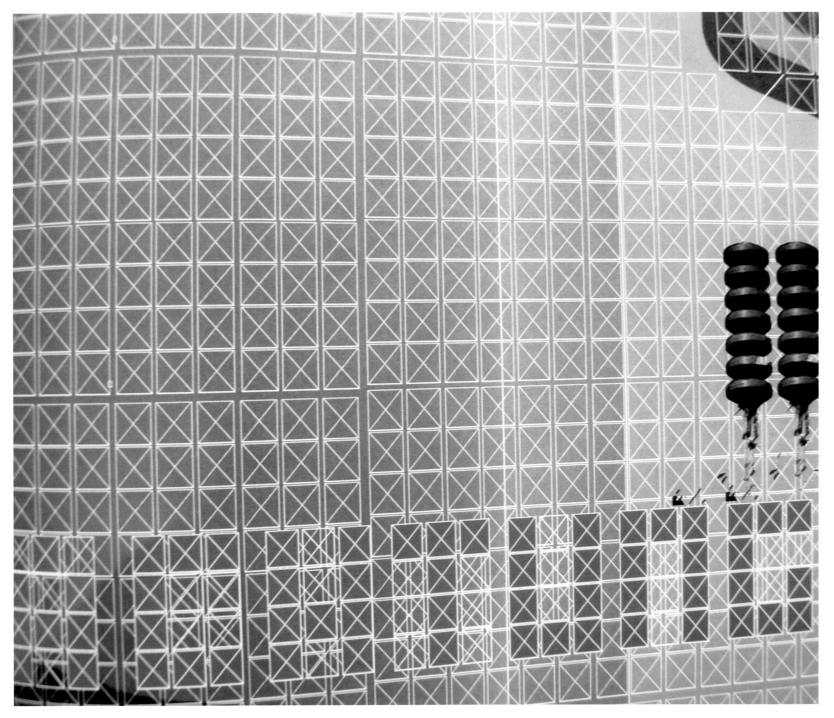

DESTINATION

ABCDEFGHIJKLMN
OPQRSTUVWXYZßÄ
ÖÜ123456789+<>

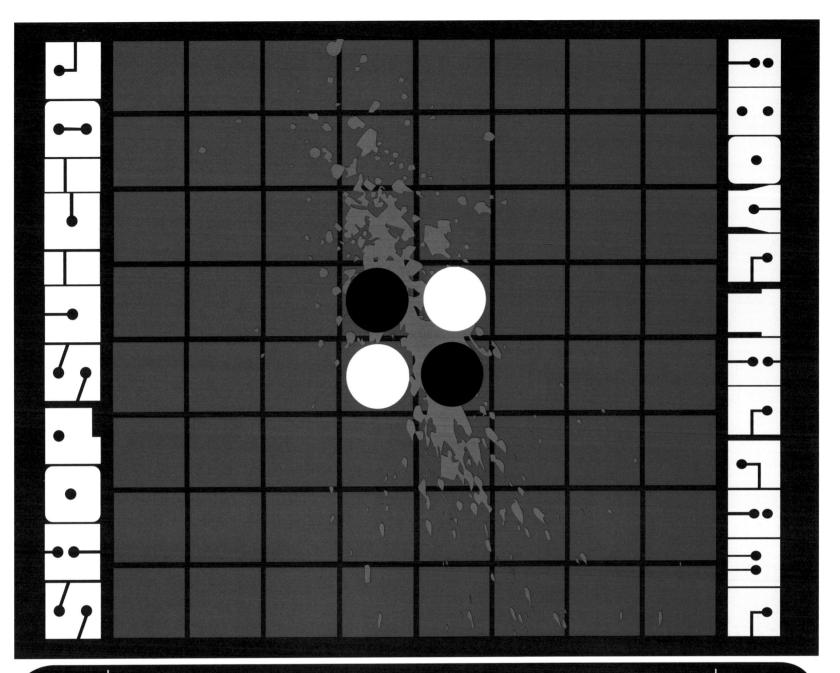

15 rue de la Chauderie 75014 Paris - be there or be square

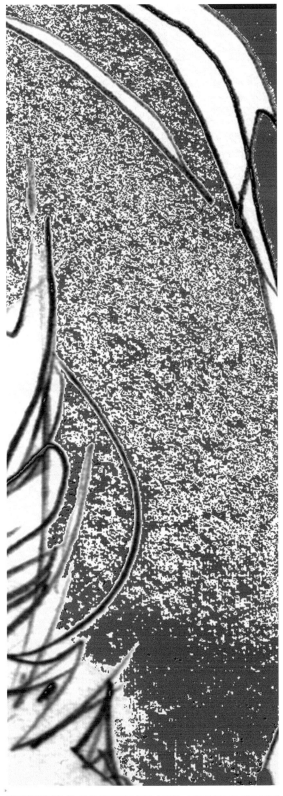

I NY

I NY

I NY

I NY

STYLE & THE FAMILY TUNES | Jammie Lidell / Jammin Unit / Poster

style @WEEK END

JAZZANOVA

DJ-Sets > Alexander Barck (Jazzanova/Sonar Kollektiv), Dirk Rumpff (OFF-Track)

ALLNIGHTLONG

23.07.05, 23h

WEEK END

Am Alexanderplatz 5, 10178 Berlin

Made possible by WEEK END OFFTRACK SONAR KOLLEKTIV style stylemag.net

GAS style @ WMF
Keep it simple.

REVOLUTION N°5 GRIME MEETS BOOTY BEATS

FEAT. KANO (679 Records, London) live
TETINE aka SLUM DUNK
(Mr Bongo, Sao Paolo) live & dj set
DANIEL HAAKSMAN (Man Records, Berlin) dj set
SICK GIRLS (WMF, Berlin) dj set GIRLS MEETS BOYS ON FRIDAY NIGHT feat. ACID MARIA & TERRIBLE

22.07.2005 ab 23h WMF Sommerlager
Rolandufer 13 U/S Jannowitzbrücke

www.sickgirls.de WMF GAS style stylemag.net
Keep it simple.

BEATSTEAKS | Smacksmash / LP / Cover Try

I ♥ NY

BEATSTEAKS

IS A KILLER

SEEED | Schwinger / Aufstehn / 12"

PART 2

illustrations : blasting off
to re-visit past missions.

Yeah, right... let's write something about Jaybo, let's write something about his illustrative work. When he first asked me if I'd like to participate and contribute to this project with a couple of lines, I was a) very flattered and b) very naive because c) I thought that this will take me a minute because I know this guy and his work for ages. But after staring at my screen for hours, I simply had to come to the conclusion that trying to describe his illustrations, prints and paintings isn't as easy as a-b-c. In fact it's a mission impossible. It's like dancing to architecture. It's like agressively fighting for peace. It's like writing tons of dialogue for a silent movie. It's like ... alright, you catch my drift. It just doesn't make any sense at all.

Don't get me wrong, it's not about nurturing my lazyness or incompetence. I just honestly think that one shouldn't always try to dissect everything, just because they can or are allowed to. I'm pretty much convinced that the majority of Jaybo's work is the result of a transcribed stream of consciousness channeled through ink, paint or a well-worn keyboard. It's a sensual thing that one should try to feel with all their senses. I mean, there's probably a reason why he's using the colours black (yes, black can be a colour) and red in a lot of his pictures. There probably is a reason why a lot of his paintings have this Asian vibe to it. Maybe it's a childhood thing, maybe he's of the opinion that things shouldn't be divided between black and white... but maybe I shouldn't clump about it as well and just sit back, relax and feel the joy of having witnessed another fine example of chilled out and multi-textured artistry instead.

Trust me on this one... you should give it a try as well.

Oh, you're feeling cheated now? Because I gave you no explainations at all, because I didn't deliver straight facts and stuff? Well, maybe it's not as important to know the answers as it is to ask the questions better. So you're trying it next time. Me, I simply didn't want to. I prefer to stick with the magic. That's next level business, dudes.

Sven 'Fortyounce' Fortmann

El Presidente

2

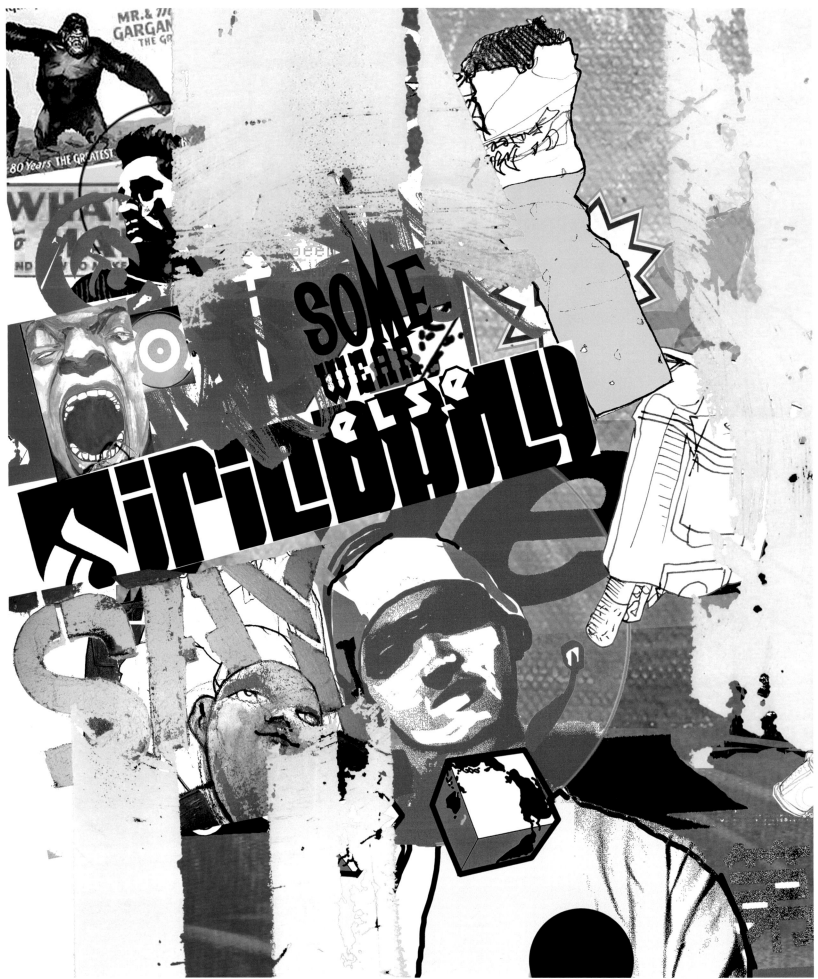

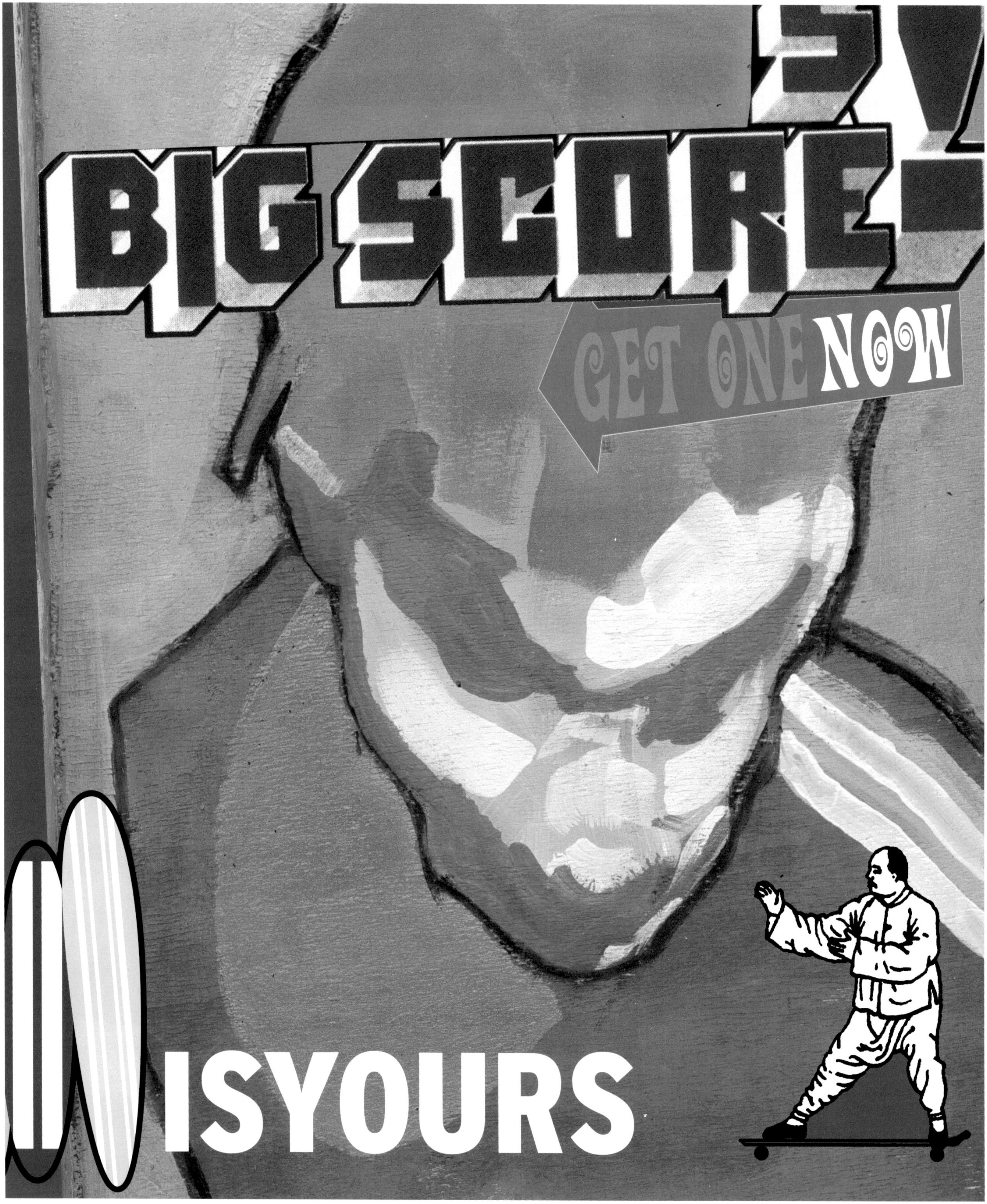
BIG SCORE
GET ONE NOW
ISYOURS

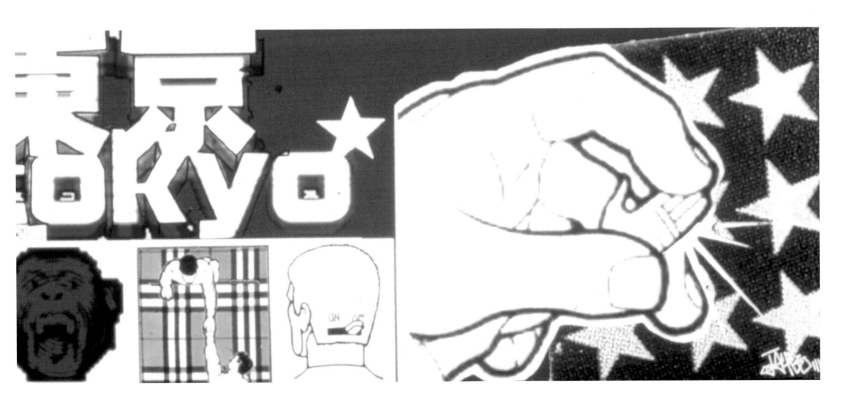

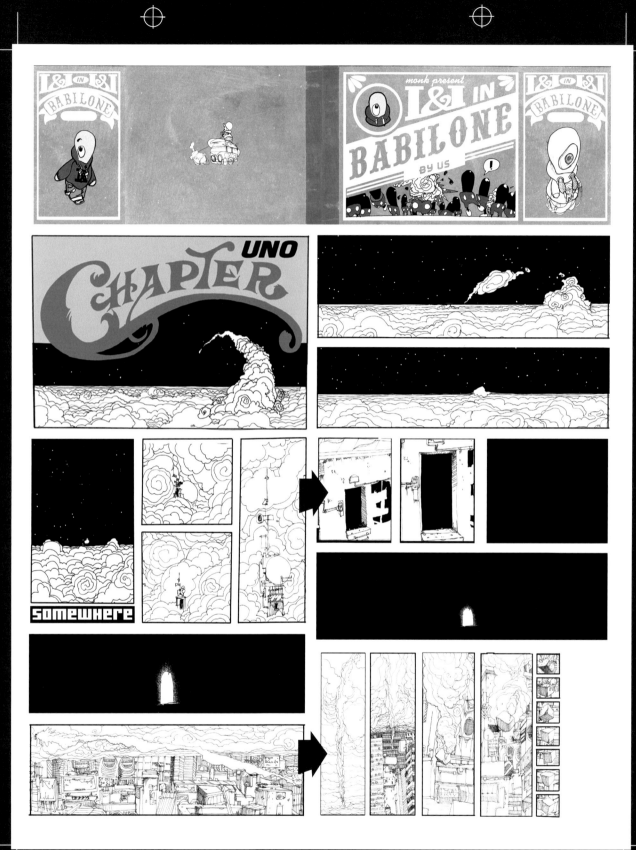

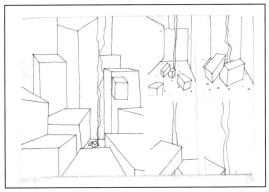

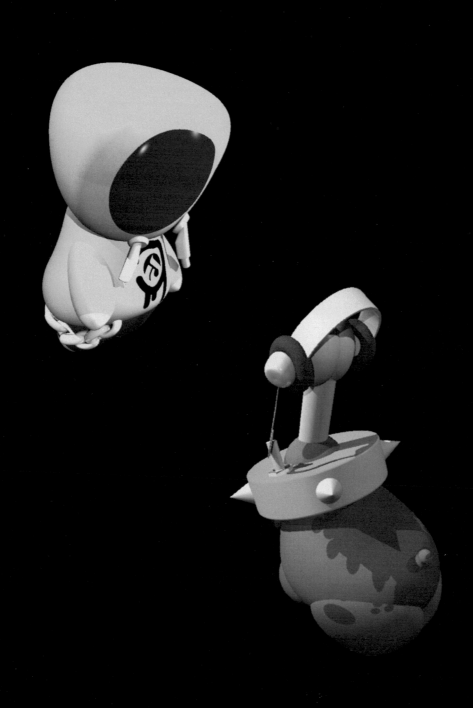

STOP WORKING... | Iriedaily

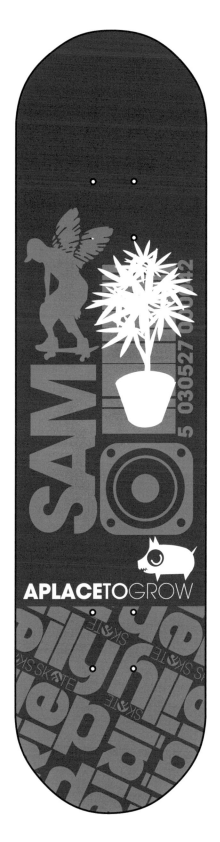

SURF NOW APOCALYPSE LATER | Iriedaily

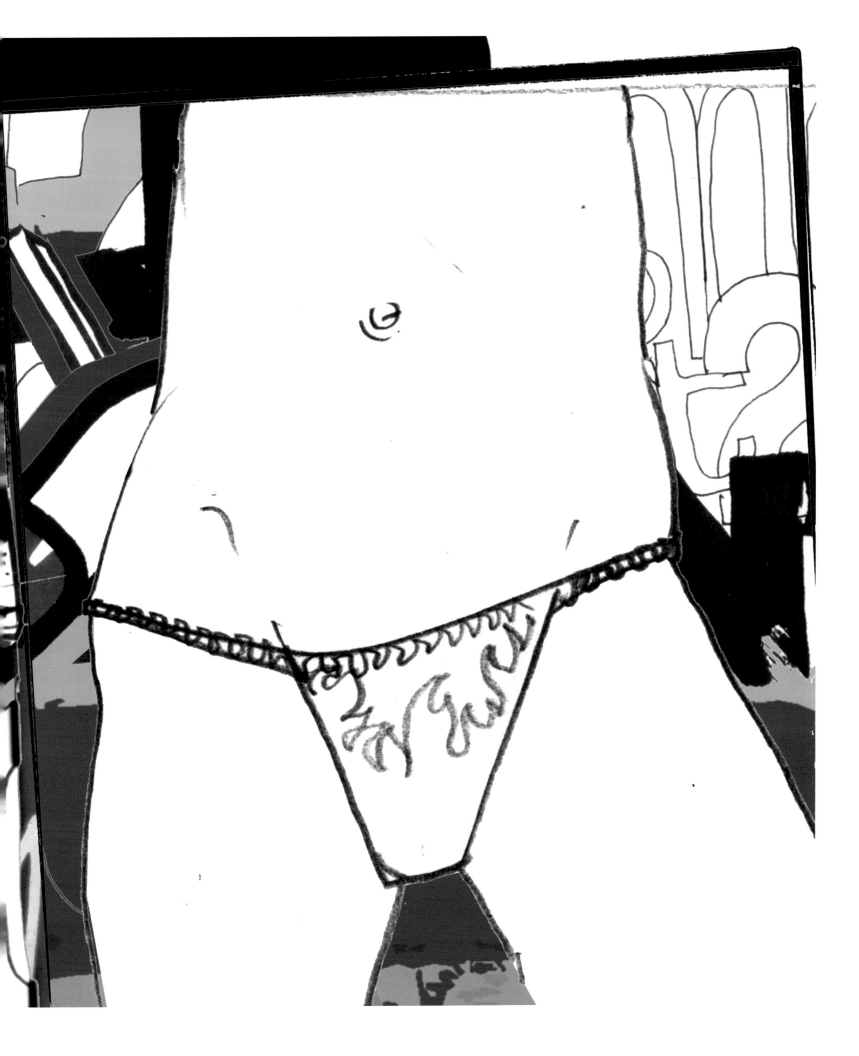

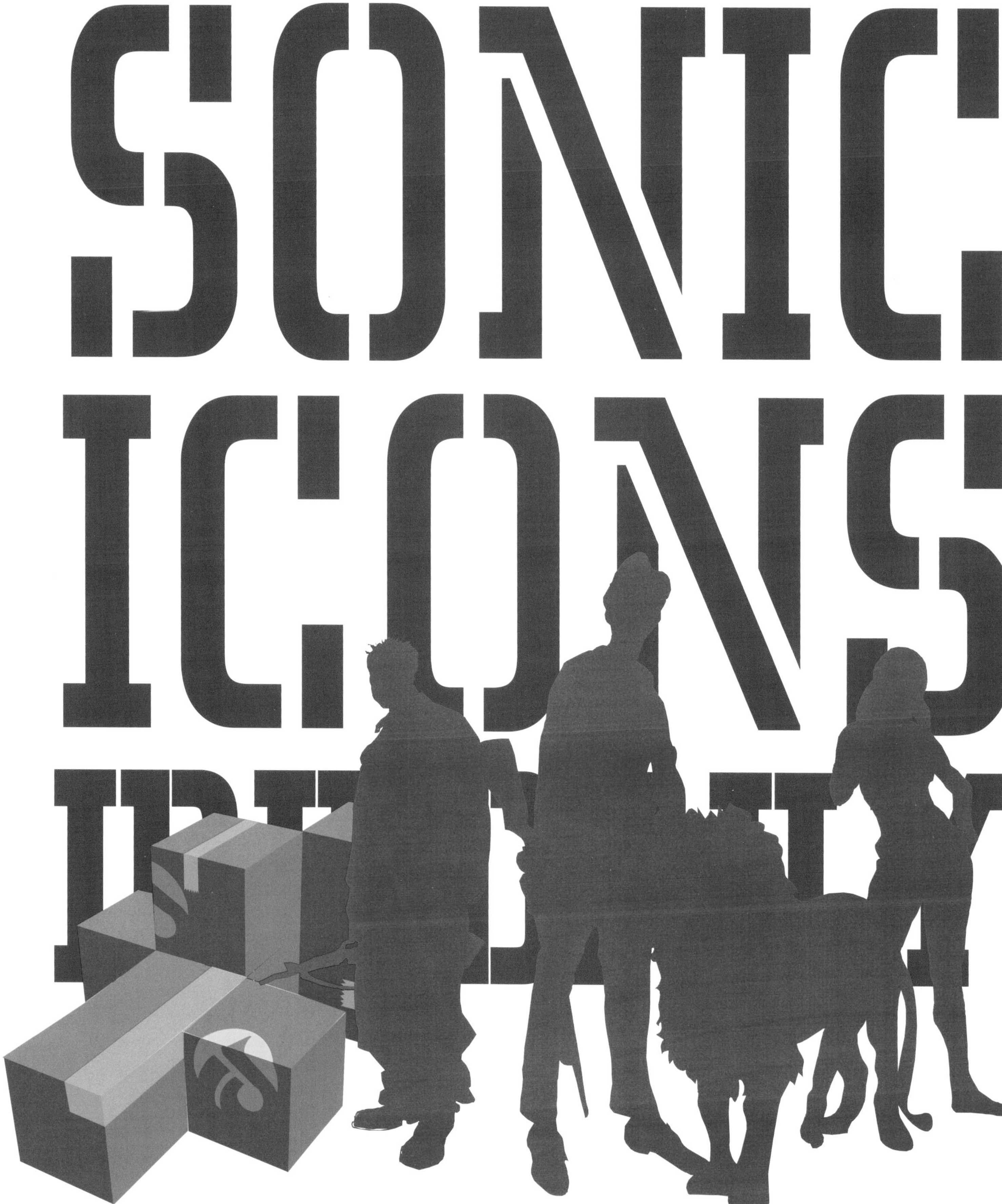
SONIC
ICONS

IRIEDAILY

IRIE SINCE94 DAILY

VENI VIDI SMOKE ONE

RIEN NE VA PLUS

AKIKO
Damura´s Dreams
神戌垂 634-8754

77

You love those weekend trips with your van
You love sweet potatoe pie when you eat it from the pan
You love to lay down on the backseat of the van
You don't sweat when the shit hit the fan
ain't that black, ain't that bad, sweet Jelly
Roll, juicy juicy soul

Cats in Bag, Bags in water, this happened at night
some dogs don't say nothing before they bite
you feel strong, because things are mooving
and the music in my bones keeps me rockin'
ain't that bad, ain't that black, sweet Jelly
Roll, bluesy juicy soul.
③

I put myself in Black 'till it's shine and glows
'till my mind gets free and my ass just follows
the darkest blues of the blue turn to blues turn to
dark, my head light rabbit is dead, in the middle
of the park. ain't that bad, ain't that black,
sweet Jelly Roll, bluesy juicy soul

Six Packs Brothers are walking in a row
drawing circles like they don't know where to go
front of your door, lo watching porn flakes on tv
we dronk too much that night, sweet dreams far
from reality, ain't that bad, ain't that black
sweet Jelly roll, lovely juicy soul

Daily News, you finally killed me, with your love
certainly. But I am happy to die if your eyes are
the last things I see. you shake your head crying
he controlled my life. Actress in tears, and I,
I exit this planet just to stay alive. ain't
that bad, ain't that black, sweet Jelly Roll,
lovely irie soul...

UP ON THE HILL FINAL

DAILY ⚫ NEWS
veni vidi smoke one

BERLIN's FINEST PICTURE NEWSPAPER

8¢
ACTION LINE
is an page 37

VOL.49 N°765 — THURSDAY MARCH 17TH. 2005 — WEATHER: THURSDAY STORMY

IRIE'S FURIOUS BREAKDOWN

In Hospital Here; Liz in Rome

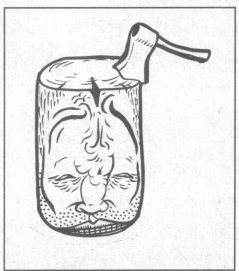

"I COULDN'T STAY ALONE"

PANIC

more on page 3

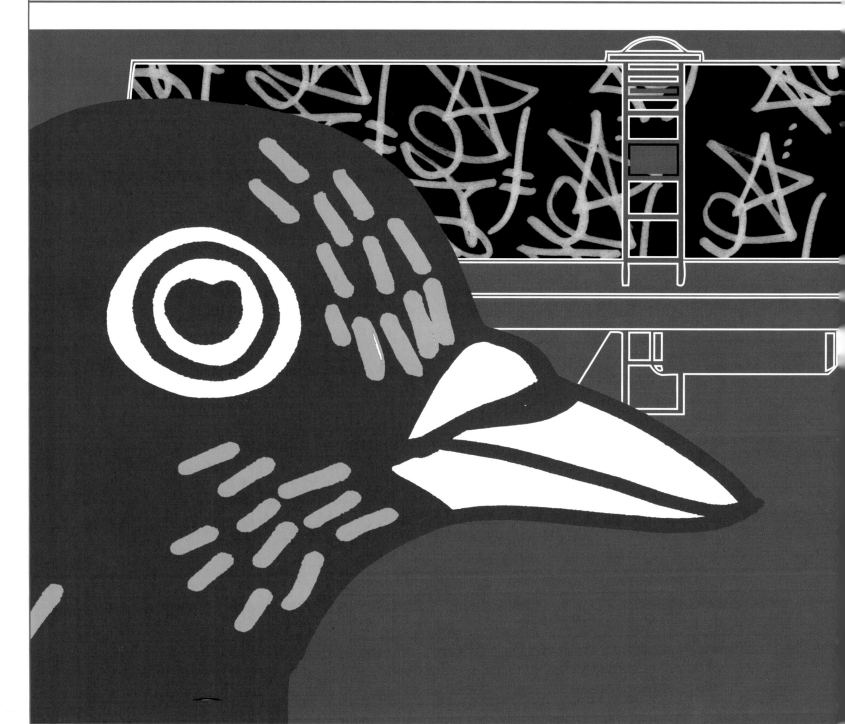

PIGEON POINT | Iriedaily

OUT OI

IRIEDAILY

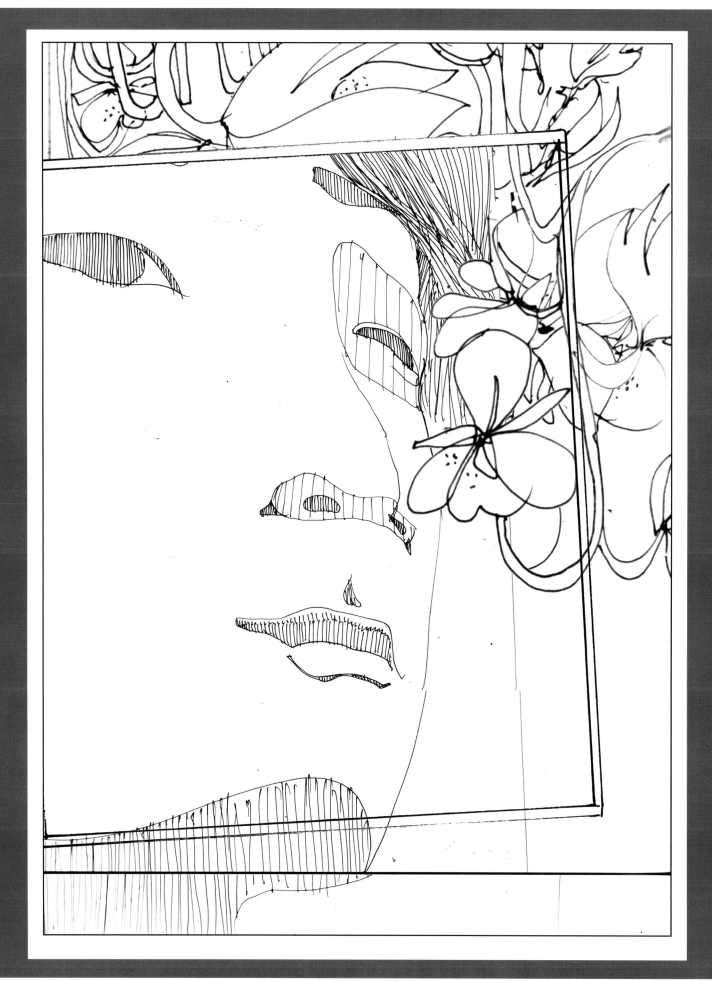

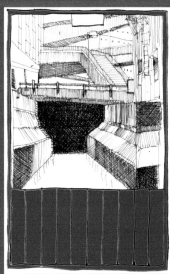

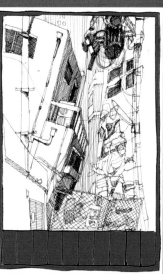

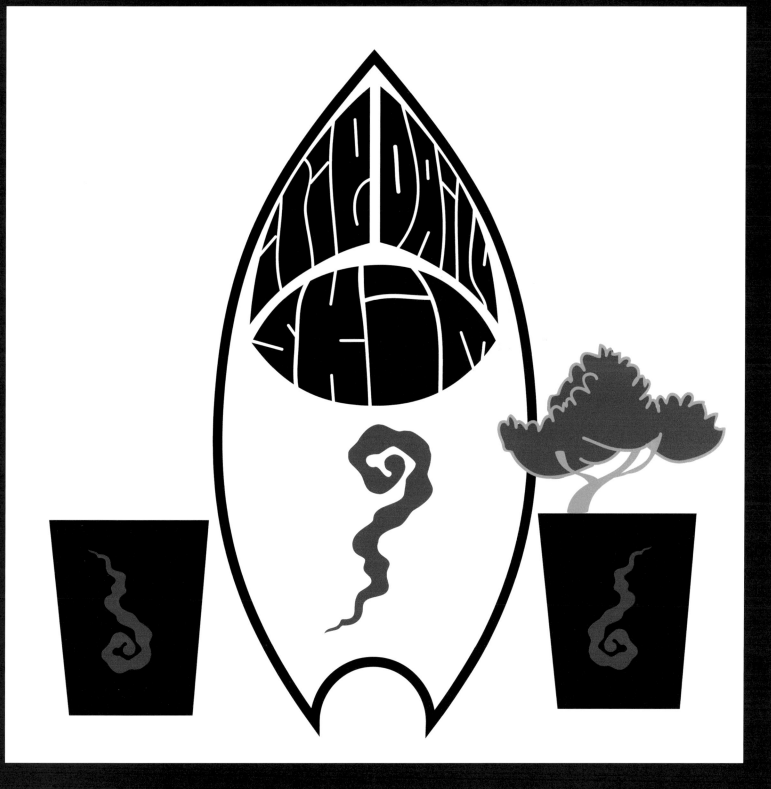

SKIM OSAKA TEAM
CARAPATEIRA· 20.07.03   PRAJA DE AMADO

General Tire:
pioneer
in rocket
power

PART3

SKRIMOV CON SHIZZNIZZ

Conceptual line feed: Talk about Monk's art direction, his creative process and his work. Involve chaos theory, insider knowledge and appreciation.

Deliver: Tomorrow.
Format: Full text. Whatever.
Start now.

TEXT SKETCH. TAKE 1
Night time (well, 11pm...), Internet sample session

If in doubt, start with chaos...

 Let´s make one thing clear. Chaos Theory is a scientific theory describing erratic "behaviour in certain nonlinear dynamical systems." That's how Wikipedia would have it and I wouldn't have it any other way, unless we are talking about Tom Clancy's "Splinter Cell - Chaos Theory." To make things worse, a Film called "Chaos Theory" was produced in the Vancouver area in January 2006, which IMDB.com describes as "a story within a story about an obsessively organized man who finds out he is sterile and that his daughter was fathered by his best friend." Oh yeah? This is no help whatsoever. And not related to anything of interest or connection here. Restart.

So, let's start over and make one thing clear, Wiki clear… "Chaos Theory deals with the behaviour of certain nonlinear dynamical systems that under certain conditions exhibit a phenomenon known as chaos. Among the characteristics of chaotic systems, described below, is a sensitivity to initial conditions (popularly referred to as the butterfly effect). As a result of this sensitivity, the behaviour of systems that exhibit chaos appears to be random, even though

the model of the system is deterministic in the sense that it is well defined and contains no random parameters. Examples of such systems include the atmosphere, the solar system, plate tectonics, turbulent fluids, economies and population growth." Now this is closer to home. That 's how it feels working here.

- Certain nonlinear dynamical systems:
Like a group of people working together maybe? In a graphic workshop or an editor's office for example? A little publishing house? A visual production agency? All of that and more rolled into one?
- Exhibiting a phenomenon known as chaos under certain conditions:
Deadline closing in, hardware malfunctioning, shortage of food supply, "my Quark cannot open your Word doc…We also want you to use the lyrics for the CD booklet, but they are not finished yet . Can we come by your house Sunday night, all 8 of us, and bring them to you, handwritten on old record company info back pages and full of corrections?" But we talked about the headline in this case not really being the headline but part of the interview quotes which is separate to the text part!" Etc., ad infinitum…
- Characteristic sensitivity to initial conditions - "butterfly effect":
4MB Ram? Mac OS2? Being dependent (of all the stuff you depend on when you´re "independent")? Butterfly my ass. Caterpillar effect is more like it, when they are still doing big-time advertising and got us into full colour printing mode!
- Seemingly random behaviour but deterministic model:
Wow, world politics now. Like the bomb that always goes off at the right time even if at the wrong place. Ever noticed that there's no "random victims" that happen to be responsible , although "random" should possibly include anybody? Makes you wonder? No? Hmm, I guess the ones killed are mostly poor idiots whose friends still yell "kill them

all" to the other side because they cannot and don't want to make an image of the profit...

The atmosphere: Your confusion, my illusion...

The solar system: The splendour of the sun, planets, moons, comets, asteroids and more.

Plate tectonics: Tectonics digging in the crates?

Turbulent fluids: Maybe you should get some medicine....

Economies: They are of scale, of scope, of density...

Population growth: Grow your own!

End of session.

TEXT SKETCH, TAKE 2
Early morning (okay, 9am...), bulked incestuous content

The writing' on the desktop!

Monk featured in French fashion magazine in 2006:
"Monk is working on his book, if and when he finds the time in between his work as the creative director of the magazine Style & The Family Tunes and as the head designer of street wear label Irie Daily, both of which he co-owns. And then there's the demand for his 'free' artwork, be it on canvas or for the sleeve designs for Berlin's bestselling acts such as Seeed or The Beatsteaks or as a spontaneous installation of paper, light and Quicktime video for a hipster gallery. Did we mention he has a private life too? Whatever, you would never guess that there is all that to be done from the relaxed manner in which Monk handles his affairs. Driving to work on his long board and playing ping pong on the conference table seem to be as much part of his modus operandi as anything he does with his PowerBook or brushes and digicam. At least he stopped doing professional music a while ago. At least for now. I hear the former rapper has learned to play the guitar since!"

Monk featured Style & The Family Tunes in 2003:
'Smoking Explosions' is the name of a group of works that Monk showed in the 'Spread Showroom' in September. The reason Monk decided to show his artworks, something which he would have preferred not to do, was his 40th birthday. The fact that Monk would prefer not to exhibit does not have anything to do with being shy. For him making art is work in progress; it is not about ending up in a gallery. There is no finished work, just a permanent evolution of output. Lines that always start anew, which are crossed over and always disappear under new picture levels. Surfaces which move simply on account of the colours and friction.
Sometimes everything is a question of the brushstroke. The symbol of the smoke, which appears as a figural element in the various works of Monk's 'Smoking Explosions' exhibition, whether drawn and painted on canvas or formed from wire as the head of an estranged toy-figure in one of the assemblages, has its roots in ancient Chinese drawing techniques. One of the ideas of these techniques is to emphasize the style of a master, so that others, perhaps students, can also copy it. Illustrators who draw comic books work in a similar way. That is how in ancient China, picture

cycles could come into being, which in detail, tell extensive stories in a certain style. That is how in the illustrated world of the comic book, a syndicate like a Marvel series involving spin-offs can come into being. A style can be established. Monk uses this technique to simultaneously work on 'versions' of his current picture-world on many different canvases – real ones or those simulated on the computer screen.

Monk used to be a graffiti artist-Tthe real thing, involving running and everything. It was fun at that time in France in the 80s. No one knew what hip-hop was, but nonetheless they understood it. In jazz improvisation it is said to be good to understand the music without comprehending it. Notes, words and scripts are bad for the flow. Monk has been in Berlin for more than 15 years now and no longer likes to run. Instead, he likes to work in his bright 200 sq. meter atelier where you can hear machines from the company next door making noise from time to time. But it is still the walls of the city that influence him. The public space that he skateboards through, the light of the region and the seasons decide the colours and give what is expressed its tone. For whoever can see it, what is appropriate for tomorrow already shows itself today in all of its nuances. Monk works on his art as creative director, designer and as co-producer of this magazine and the fashion company Irie Daily. But the decisive influence comes from freelance work. A clear unwavering eye and ideally carried out strokes do not get along well with deadlines and 'brand worlds.. Feelings are stronger than products and are not always nice, modern or convenient. And they are not something that can be bought. Many pictures by street artists scream so loud that everyone has to hear it. In Monk's work, everything also always looks good. A scream from Northern Europe, like one of a Frenchman longing for a better world with more beautiful weather generates.

The series of works 'Smoking Explosions' has three figural elements. The 'smoke,' is Monk's adaptation of Chinese cloud painting, a burning match and empty speech balloons. The clouds were added in September 2001. Since then, Monk has felt that he has been accompanied by a new aesthetic of explosions, flames and smoke which has penetrated the scenario of the media reality on the TV news; that scared Monk and hurt the pictures. Perhaps the smoke will never stop. The match symbolizes life. Half burnt, but still half there. Like the glass, the chalice. Life at 40. The speech balloons are an image for the speechlessness of humanity as Monk perceives it. 'Language has subjected me to too many lies. Conversation is hard for me. I've heard too many lies; I stopped trusting words when I was a child.' The language of Monk's images uses clear elements, which remain naive and thereby establish a framework, freeing the actual forms of expression from the tasks of picture composition. The language of graphic design, comicbook style and pop. 'I try to create a dialogue. I use symbols that have stories, like a James Dean photo or an Andy Warhol soup can and want to show their development.' The pictures are fundamentally about the artist's own self-portraits and perceptions, the unconsciously emerging, coincidental elements, colours and forms. 'The

surfaces are more important than the lines. I'm looking for vibrating colours. Next to the brown, the blue almost has a neon-like effect, although it is only chalk blue, a summer sky. There is a play with the center. An avoidance of the center.' Next to the creative levels, there are contents. Fleeting things. Things that cannot properly be verbalized. Sensual things. In his art, Monk works on what he has experienced. The pictures are like diaries, commentaries; their emergence has a mood, reflects the spirit of the day and involves evolution. Their quality is almost temporary, as if they would pass away like the organic works of Andy Goldsworthy. While this man finds his material and dynamic in nature, Monk has a vocabulary that is characterized by a flood of images and material excess. He has to create in the rhythm of a 'civilized' environment, the one of Berlin, Europe, the 21st century.

The use of indefinite, unintentional elements involves a method. Sometimes it 'has to do with the digit 3,' then ghostly Asian faces are simply added. I'm not always the master of the situation, sometimes I fall in love with a stroke, a line and want to repeat it. Then it is about keeping a balance in the whole thing. That's also what happens when I design Style.' For Irie in the meantime that's different. There I would have liked to have continued just making T-shirts, really extreme ones, but the market does not want that. For me T-shirts are the most beautiful canvas in the world. That also has to do with the fact that there's always a person who wears it, which is very interesting. But in the meantime at Irie Daily we are working on a whole lifestyle, that's not just me alone...' The reality of daily bread and butter jobs involves a lack of freedom as its condition. Something always has to becompleted by a certain deadline, otherwise the production process would not work. Without deadlines, there would be no newspaper, just the endless development of layouts. And then at Style and Irie there are the others, those whose opinions also play a role. There, one cannot avoid compromises; one is not the only author. When Monk only works for himself, different rules are valid. In 'Smoking Explosions' this can be seen in that he prefers not to generate an end result and let an exhibition or the status quo into the flow of his work. 'I paint the images that I already have inside me. The explosions take place in my head. When painting, I jump between various pictures on which I am simultaneously working. They are evidence of a certain time; the pictures consist of situations. A monkey emerges, then another one. It's like a lab. The pictures are repeatedly painted over and are never finished. To understand the pictures one has to see them more than once, one has to see how they emerge. I work on the pictures until they are taken away for an exhibition or until someone comes and buys one or something like that happens. When a picture is gone, for me it is almost dead; it no longer exists. I can no longer see it. But when I then do see it, I only see the mistakes, those which I should have done differently. I always put everything into question, regardless of how good it is. I always ask myself if there is something better.' It is the 'errors,' the imperfection, which are responsible for the emergence of a trademark in Monk's pictures and works.

Monk not only does pictures, but also builds and works on objects and sometimes even programs computer animation. 'Animation is a very involved medium, painstaking because I do it alone. To date, I haven't been able to stop working on it. I like to experiment. The whole multitasking and being occupied with completely different materials is all the same work for me. Sometimes I need a hammer, sometimes a brush. For me animation has a lot to do with music, with rhythm. Music is also something which I like doing. I play the guitar like an idiot.' Output is everything, but what he likes best is drawing or painting. 'In an empty room I'd paint with blood. It's a compulsion. If I don't do it for a long time I go crazy. I need output.' Monk collects material for his assembled objects. What's exciting? 'I voluntarily go there. To the flea market. Or also buy expensive things to make something out of them. If I have a set idea, sometimes I look for something but can't find it. Instead, I find something else that I can use and I make something new with it. An evolution. Until it has been done.' The possibility to work 'in 3-D' in a larger scale, came when Irie Daily became convinced that at a trade fair stand, no clothes need to be visible. For a year now, Monk has been able to arrange and work on the assemblages in his 'Spread Space' at Style. In the past two years Monk designed two trade fair stands, which developed an artistic life of their own. They are spatial constructs, architecture that is in constant movement, based on boxes, which, with objection, are equipped and decorated. 'These objects in turn show the pictures, the things, which were important for me at the time they came into being.'
And what happens when the 'Smoking Explosions' are completely exhibited and 'exposed?' When their figures have to make room for new space? Everything will be different or perhaps not. Monk himself does not know. 'At some point the old works become sediments, humus. But things go forward. The only things that return are the changing comicbook styles. Sometimes Marvel, then Manga again. I'm currently inspired by Europeans like Hergé as well as by the Asians.'
Sometimes Monk's schedule gets really tight, because the timing and flow have to agree. The main thing is that there is enough space. 'I like to be in the flow but not necessarily with it. I don't want to go against the flow, but I also don't just want to be pulled along. I need space.' A pause, stopping is not an option; Monk very much needs the output. 'I will only be finished on the day that I die.'''

Note: The "Spread Space" is no longer. Monk´s atelier is now a former roof builder's studio full of old timber and debris.
Also Note: I stumbled across a cardboard box the other day, near Monk´s desk. The box had a face painted on it that seemed strangely familiar, although I hadn't seen it (or it's brothers...) before. Big deal, after some time, this is bound to happen, when you have to acquaint yourself with an artist's signature. But it wasn't the deja vu type sensation that struck me. It was the personal relation I felt to the image. You see, some of my best friends are images. Monk´s images.
Dr.B.Lunt, March 2006

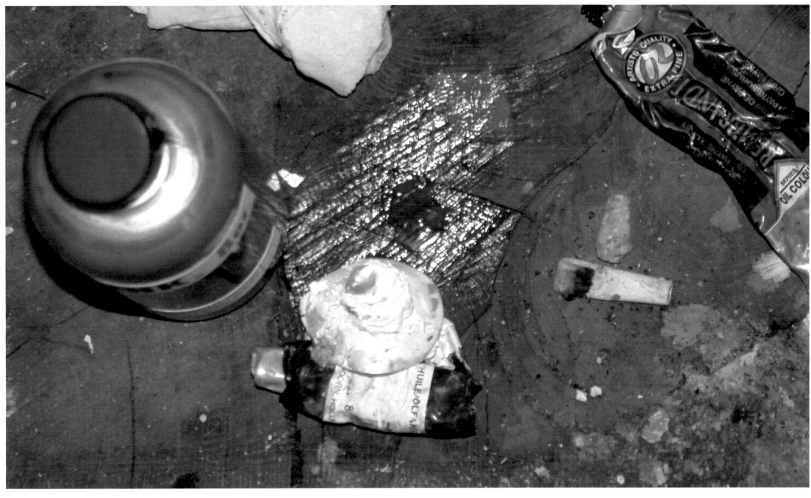

ZEN GARDEN | Style Installation / Detail

MISS PLUME | Toy Prototype

TOYS PROTOTYPE | Monkimons **MAMBO DOG** | Monkimons

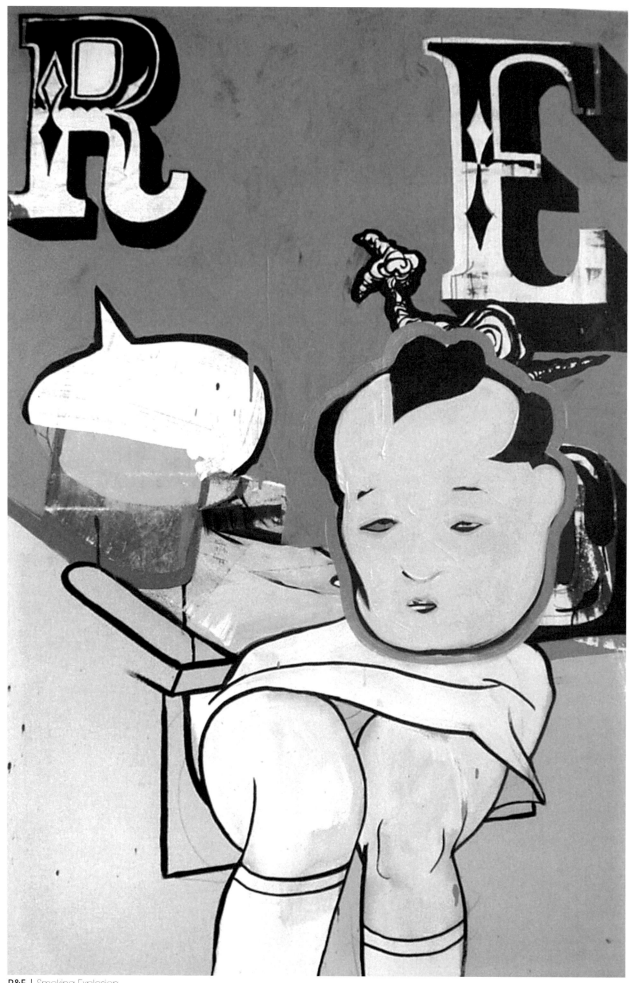

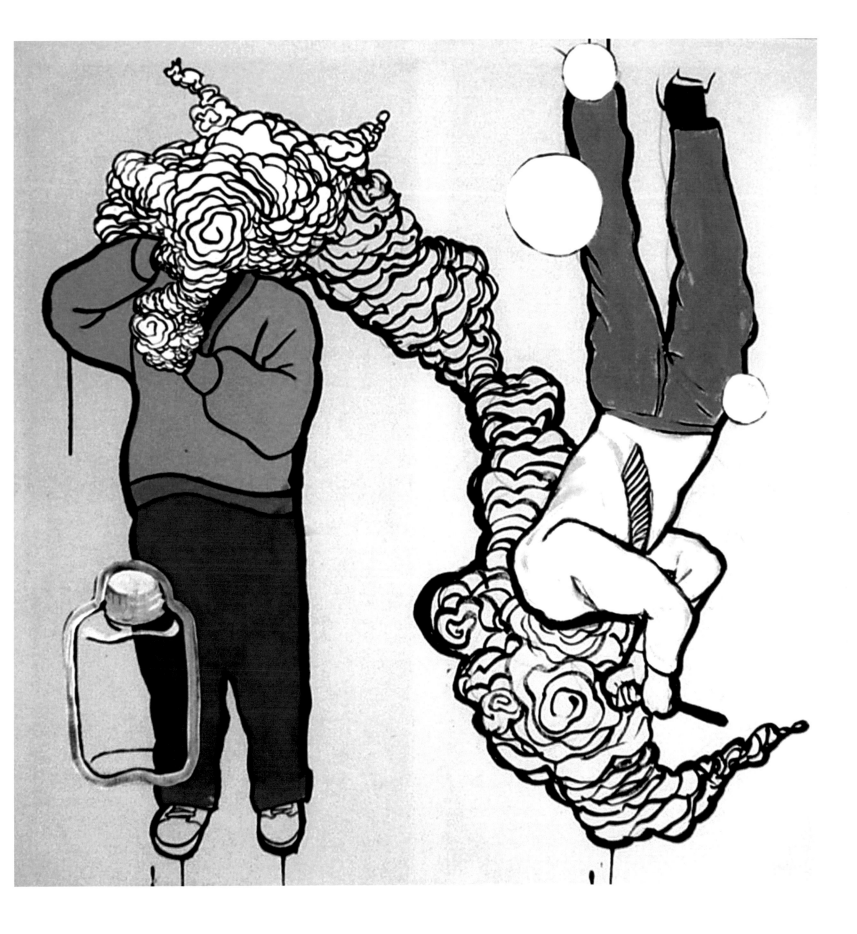

DOC JUSTICE

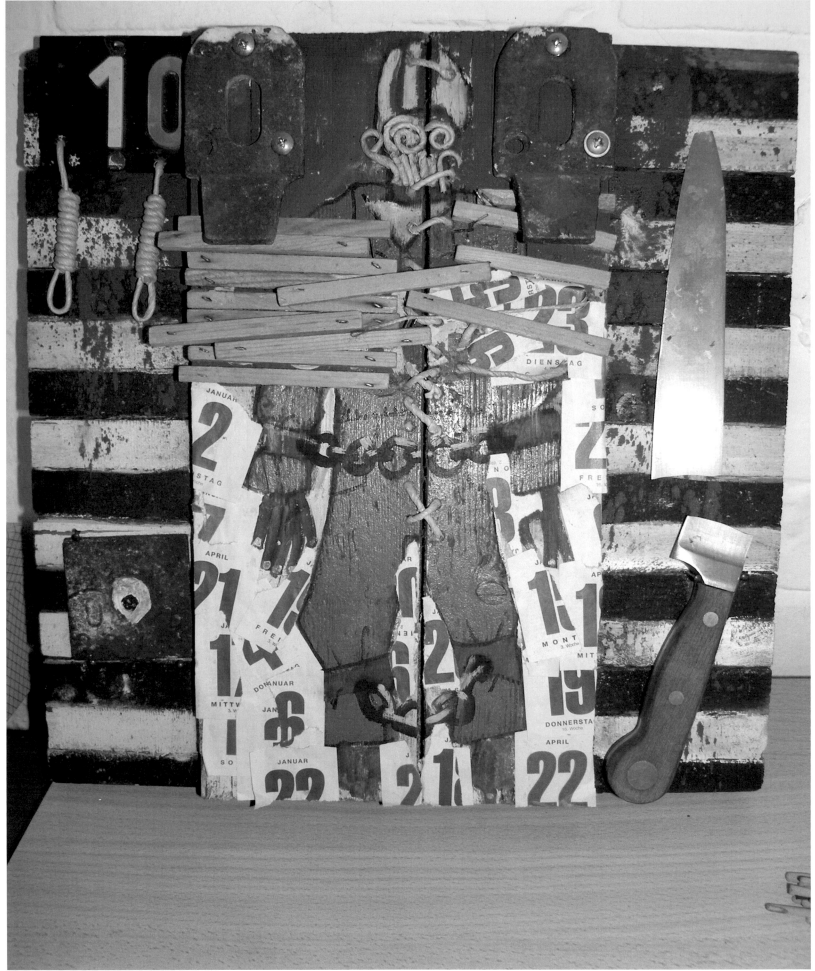

LOSING MY TIME

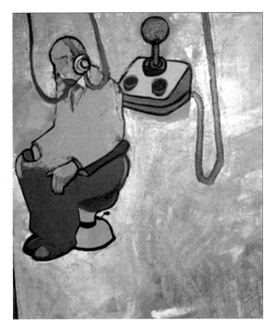

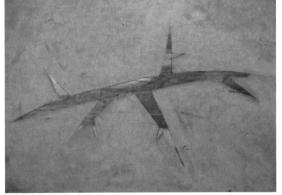

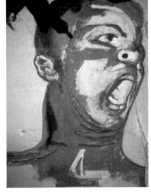

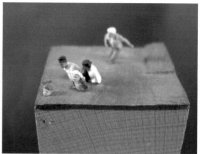

STOP MAKING SENSE | Stan Smith Anniverary @ Foot Locker   **BOOM BALLERINA** | Miss Goodnight   **WALKING LUCK** | Superfly Exhibit   **THE END** | Pf Flyer Custom   **SINKING** | SuperFly Exhibit

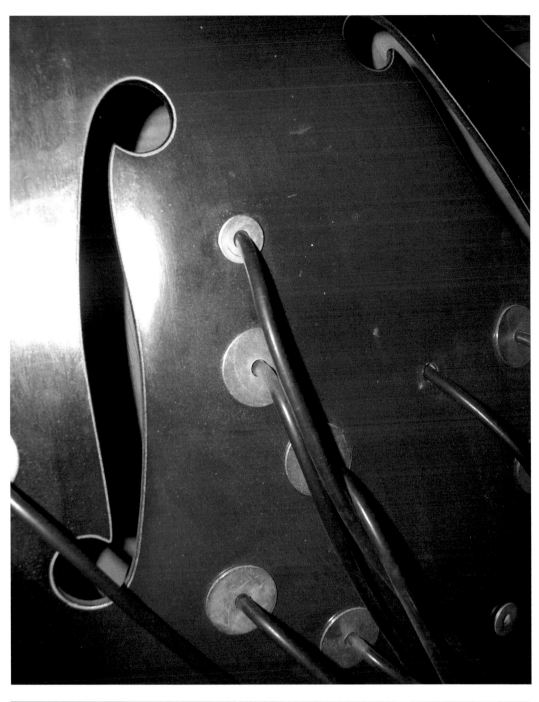

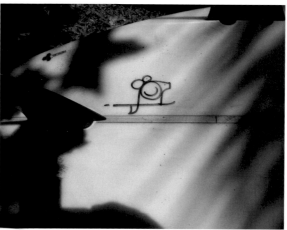

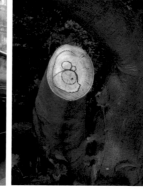

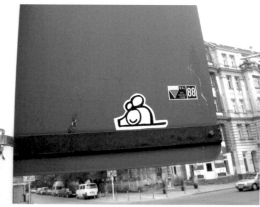

MISTAH PHONE | Spread Visuals   **MAO-MAM** | Iriedaily Stand   **OT OF MY NAME** | Shoe Ting

SMOKING EXPLOSION | Fighting with Myself   **IRIE DEM SOUL SYSTEM** | Iriedaily Spray Cans

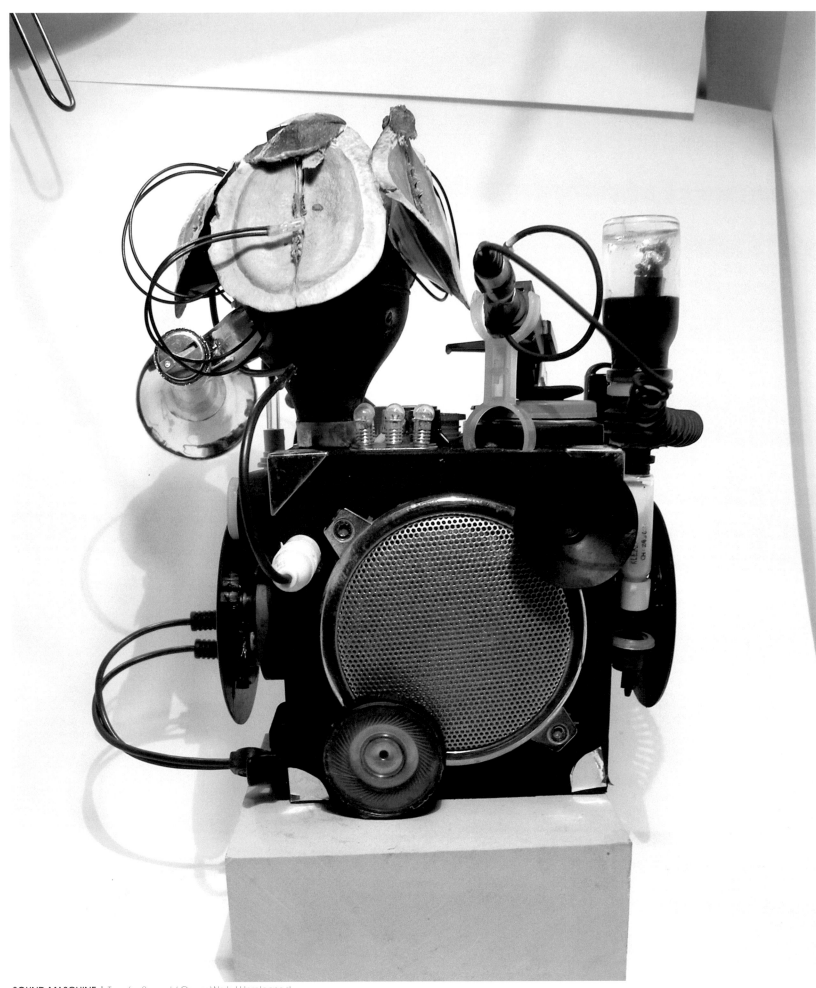

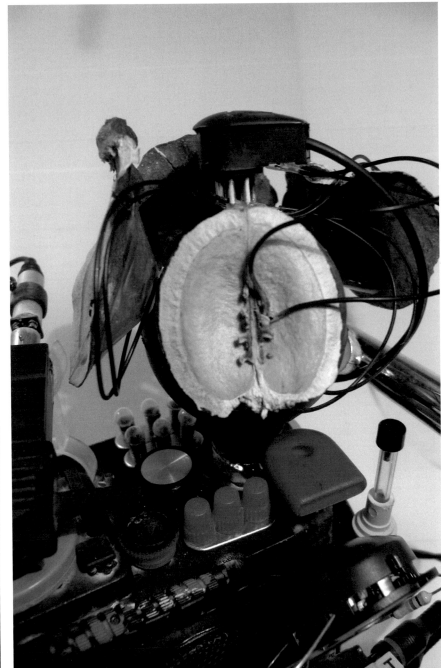

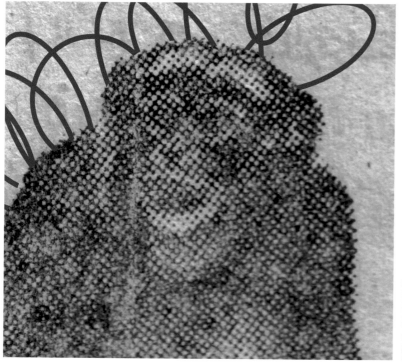

T8O 3ONⱯEY
SANE SANE THEY
ARE ALL INSANE
- THE FIREMAN'2
  BLIND THE CONDUCTOR'S
  LANE. A SPANISH
  MONKEY AND A SAD
  LUCK DAME.
  HANGING OUT THE
  WINDOW WITH A
  BOTTLE FULL OF
  RAIN.

UNAI PARA JBO
TODO POR NADA.
2007

RASTERMONKEY 1,2,3 | *Monk / Words by Anton Unai*

TIERGARTEN | BBB Iriedaily Messe Stand Cast.

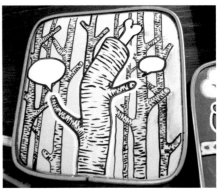

MY HEAD IS MY HOUSE | Monk for Heinrich Nikolaus

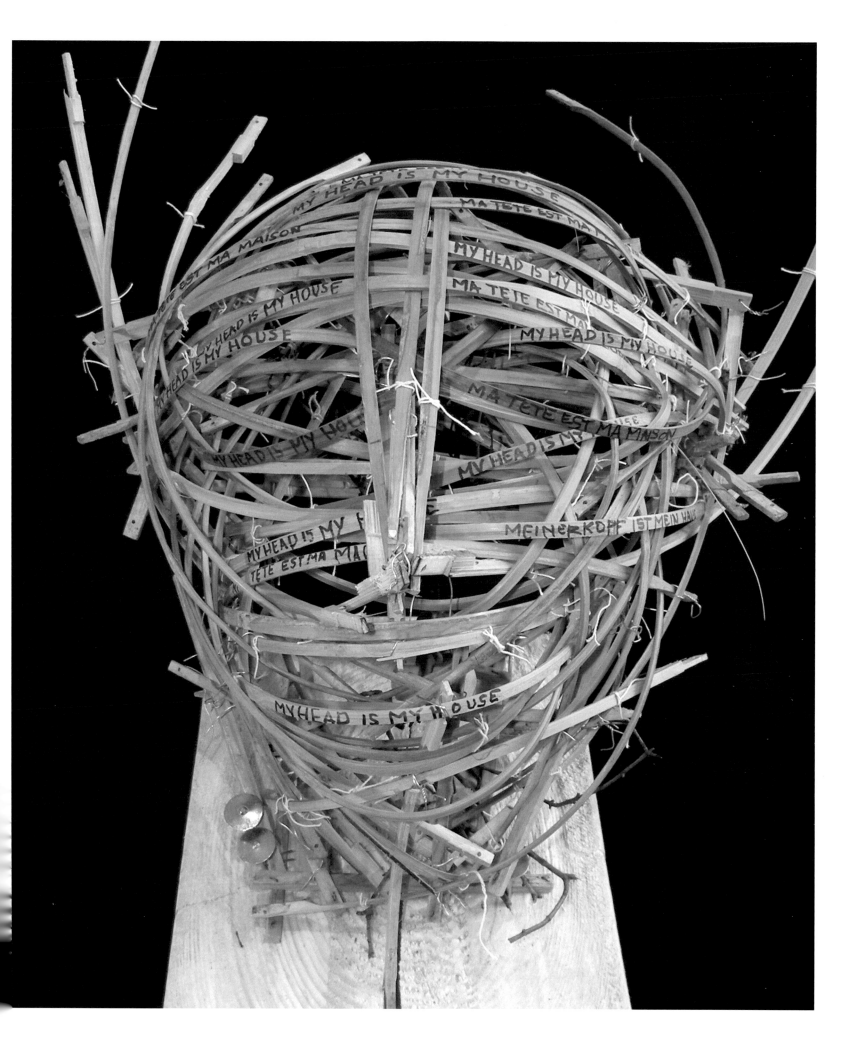

WHITESHADOWS

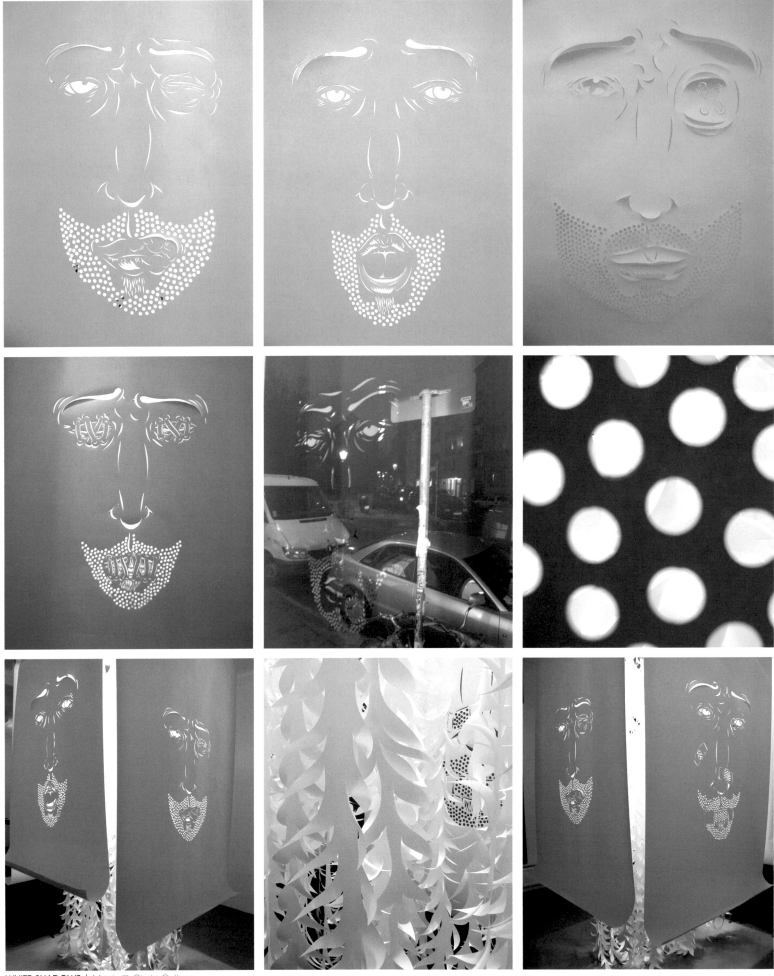

WHITE SHADOWS | Monk @ Circle Culture

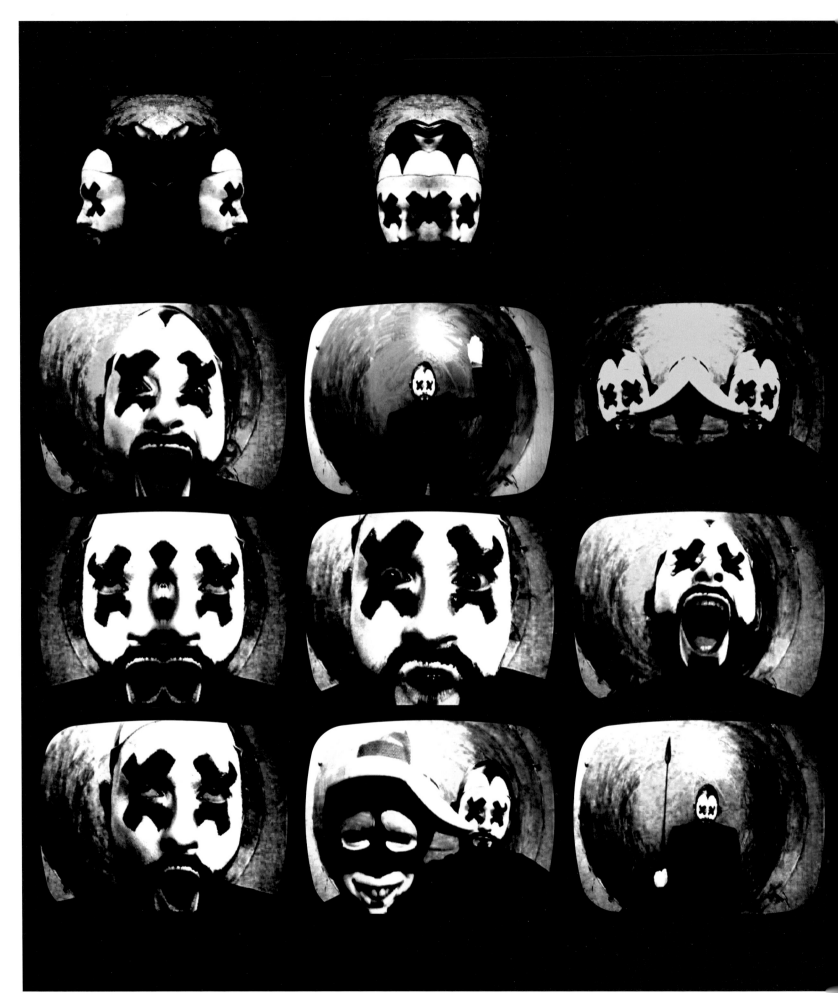

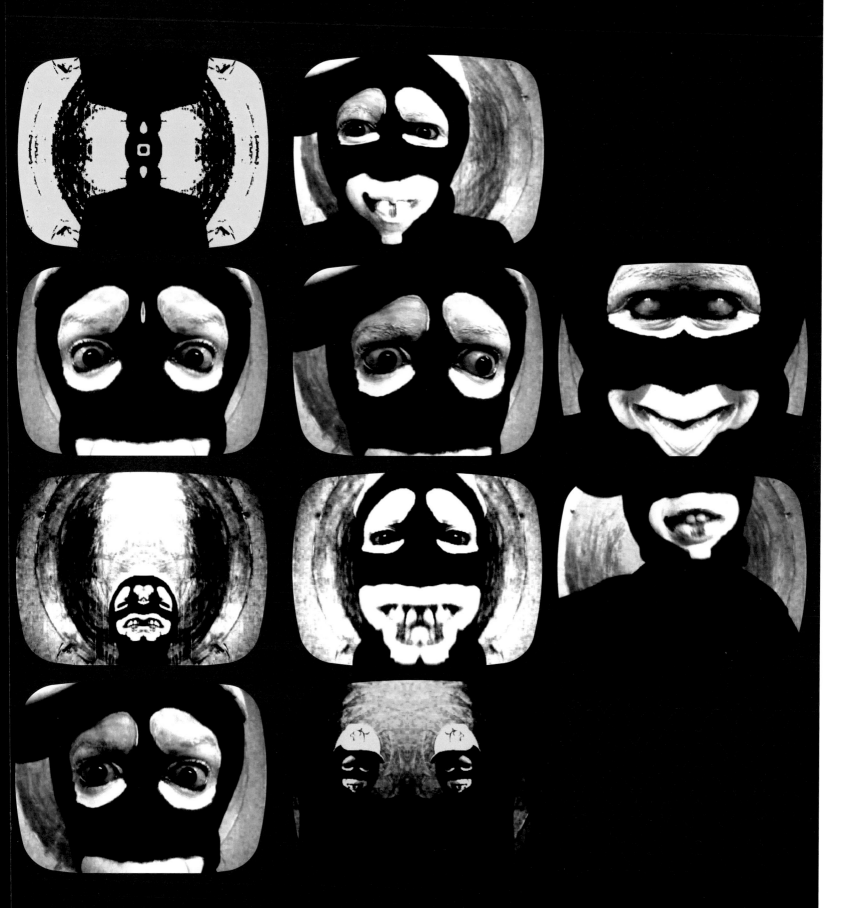

CARAPATEIRA | Praia De Amado

This is for those who make everything possible! Big XXXL thanks to Cathy and Manou for your maximum support during those hard days of making this book, for always giving your precious love. I love you and I will always love you. Thanks to the spread visuals crew, Sina, Marie, Henne, who keep my head up when the job wave was too big. Thanks to the Style and The Family Tunes Posse who make me believe in what I do, special thanx to Dr. B.Lunt - master of the word, Antje, Betty, Kitty, Ole, Olli, Katharina, Frank, Violetta, Flo, Jana, Schnurps. Thanks to the Iriedaily Crew for believing in me through all these years, especially Daniel for keeping my two feet on the floor, Walt, Man, Ant, Mario, Pierre, Bella, Paty, Denise, Bindo, Sam, Bakari, Jürgen, Maxym, Mäxx, Rolle, Mario, Tibor. Thanks to my building crew, Eynar, Idefix, Rehagel. Thanx to Kreuzberg for having me, Remo, Ines, Eric, Stefan, Rita, Radio Arne, Chiggy, Nelly, Karin, Ringo, Peterchen, Zeze, Zézé, The Hawkings, Jörg "Terrible", Alexandra, Sick Girls, Heike Summ-Ze-Man, Jörg Suermann, Petal, Tyron Ricketts, Seeed, Demba, Pierre, Frank, Tobsten, Thorsten, Jérome, Basty, Beatsteaks Arnim, Tomate, Zolle, Maggie, Jah Fish, Mellowbag, B-side, Daniel Harder, Dejoe, Caskoe, Pfadfinderei, Walter Medialis, Circle Culture, Johann, Nadine, Ulrike and the girls, Rudi l'africain, Marilène del Tessino, Heinrich Nikolaus, Sawan "wo ist mein skateboard?", WMF, Gerriet, Husito, Frank Gerritz, Astrid Grosser, Frank Thiel, Lowdown, Marok, Hesse, Paninologie, no food, no coffe, no book, Paolo, Irene, a big phat one to my inspiration master Anton Unai heart core. Barcelona, Pez, Xupete, Cha noir, 1980's Aism, Jean und Christine Verdier. Thanx to the writers of this book: Isi, 40oz, B.Lunt for letting their minds rock on my chaos. Thanks to the photographers of this book: Artoo, Andy Rumble, EmBe, ... Thanx to Die Gestalten, Robert, Markus, Andreas for giving me this chance. And this one goes out to the one I forgot, even if your name is not mentioned I will never forget what you did for me. At least but not last a big thought to Daniel, R.I.P, rest in Power, may the waves be with you!
And a special extra phat for the one and only EmBe / Martin Bretschneider.

www.stylemag.net   www.iriedaily.de   www.spread.de

Lord of Mess – my head is a visual township

by Jaybo aka Monk
Layout by Jaybo aka Monk

Production by Martin Bretschneider/dgv
Text corrections by Kitty Bohlhöfer & Lina Kunimoto/dgv
Printed by Graphicom Srl., Vicenza
Published by Die Gestalten Verlag, Berlin 2006
ISBN 3-89955-154-0

Bibliographic information published by Die Deutsche Bibliothek
Die Deutsche Bibliothek lists this publication in the Deutsche Nationalbibliografie;
detailed bibliographic data is available in the Internet at
http://dnb.ddb.de.

For more information please check: www.die-gestalten.de

Respect copyright, encourage creativity!